Crisis Stability and Nuclear Exchange Risks on the Subcontinent

Crisis Stability and
Nuclear Exchange Risks on the Subcontinent
Major Trends and the Iran Factor

By Thomas F. Lynch III

Institute for National Strategic Studies
Strategic Perspectives, No. 14

Series Editor: Nicholas Rostow

National Defense University Press
Washington, D.C.
November 2013

For current publications of the Institute for National Strategic Studies, please visit the NDU Press Web site at: www.ndu.edu/press/index.html.

Contents

Executive Summary

Crisis stability—the probability that political tensions and low-level conflict will not erupt into a major war between India and Pakistan—is less certain in 2013 than at any time since their sequential nuclear weapons tests of 1998. India's vast and growing spending on large conventional military forces, at least in part as a means to dissuade Pakistan's tolerance of (or support for) insurgent and terrorist activity against India, coupled with Pakistan's post-2006 accelerated pursuit of tactical nuclear weapons as a means to offset this Indian initiative, have greatly increased the risk of a future Indo-Pakistani military clash or terrorist incident escalating to nuclear exchange.[1] America's limited abilities to prevent the escalation of an Indo-Pakistani crisis toward major war are best served by continuing a significant military and political presence in Afghanistan and diplomatic and military-to-military dialogue with Pakistan well beyond 2014.

Iranian acquisition of a nuclear weapons capability will not directly affect the ongoing erosion of crisis stability in South Asian. However, a declared or a declared and tested nuclear Iranian weapons capability almost certainly will inspire Saudi Arabia's acquisition of its own nuclear deterrent and involve Pakistan. If American efforts to halt Iran or to extend acceptable deterrence to Riyadh fail, then Washington must accept that Islamabad will transfer some form of nuclear weapons capability to Saudi Arabia as part of the Kingdom's pursuit of an autonomous nuclear deterrent versus Tehran. Washington's best policy option is to maintain sufficient diplomatic and military relevance in Islamabad and Riyadh to limit transfer impact upon Israel's threat calculus and to constrain Gulf-wide proliferation that could excite Indian fears for its nuclear deterrent in a manner that stokes a presently dormant nuclear arms race between India and China.

Introduction

Since the mid-1970s, and especially since 1998, volumes have been written about nuclear weapons proliferation in Pakistan and India and the impact of this proliferation on stability and security on the Subcontinent.[2] Other literature has focused on the manner in which decisions about strategic force structures in Pakistan, India, China and the United States connect to one another in discrete nuclear proliferation chains, driving decisions that impact an interconnected set of paired security dilemmas (Pakistan-India and India-China, India-China and China-U.S.).[3] Over the past decade, a legion of authors and commentators have made considerable speculation about the security risks from Iran's nuclear program and the risks that program poses for crisis stability and nuclear weapons incentives in the Persian Gulf and between Iran and its Arab neighbors.[4]

This monograph aims to update and integrate these three areas of analysis. It updates the status of nuclear weapons proliferation and crisis stability on the Subcontinent as of early 2013. It also explores the relationship between Iran's nuclear development trajectory and pathways, discussing the interplay of Saudi Arabia and Pakistan in the context of possible responses to Iran's nuclear program endstate. It then discusses the most likely security impacts from Saudi-Pakistan interaction on nuclear weapons collaboration for South Asian nuclear stability and proliferation dynamics. Finally, it discusses the implications for American policymakers desiring to counteract the worst-case possibilities foretold by these interactions: spiraling Indo-Pakistani military crises and escalating arms races between India, China, and Pakistan on the Subcontinent.

India and Pakistan: The Dominant Nuclear and Security Realities

There are three classic formulations of stability in relation to nuclear weapons and the propensity for war. The first, *"first strike" stability* (or *"deterrence" stability*), is defined as the presence of an assured second strike capability for each nuclear-armed party in a confrontation such that each fears unacceptable retaliatory damage should a nuclear exchange occur.[5] *"Crisis stability"* is defined as a condition in which neither side fears initiation of an armed clash—nuclear, conventional, or subconventional (including a preemptive strike against nuclear assets)—in the event of an interstate political crisis either because of the presence of a comprehensive first strike defense or other impracticability. Finally, *"arms race" stability* accrues when neither side has concerns that its adversaries might build weapons that undermine stability by achieving a technological breakthrough or a clandestine build-up of force that produces decisive battlefield advantage.[6]

Historically, the debate about nuclear weapons and stability on the Subcontinent has centered on the notion of "crisis stability"—the incentives for either side to strike a first blow with its array of forces: nuclear, conventional, or irregular militias and terrorists. Secondarily, it has focused on the topic of "arms race" stability.

From 1999 to 2010, two distinct viewpoints developed about the relationship between nuclear weapons proliferation and crisis stability between the historic South Asian antagonists.[7] An "optimist" perspective asserted that nuclear proliferation had reduced the threat of conventional conflict and major war. The "pessimist" position contended that the proliferation of nuclear weapons had increased the frequency of low-intensity, but significant, armed clashes mainly instigated by the activities of militia forces and terrorists and that these subconventional clashes increased the risk of escalation to major conventional warfare and nuclear war.[8]

Pessimists believed that the presence of nuclear weapons did briefly erode crisis stability at the conventional level of conflict. Citing the summer 1999 Kargil crisis—the first military stand-off between Indian and Pakistan subsequent to their 1998 nuclear weapons tests—pessimists argued that the Pakistani military was emboldened by its perceived nuclear symmetry with India. This led then–Pakistani Army Chief of Staff General Pervez Musharraf to initiate a conventional attack near Kargil in Jammu-Kashmir in the belief that India dared not escalate conventionally given the Pakistani nuclear deterrent. While this gambit failed due to political intervention,[9] pessimists more generally contended that the record demonstrated that Pakistan chose an anti-India policy of increasing the frequency of low-intensity conflict, particularly that incited by insurgents and terrorists in Jammu-Kashmir and across India, both before and after the May 1998 nuclear weapons tests, in the belief that India dared not retaliate due to the Pakistani bomb.[10]

Using canonical Cold War nuclear deterrence logic, a second viewpoint countered that the presence of nuclear weapons on the Subcontinent actually enhanced crisis stability by discouraging risk-taking between conventional military forces. Scholars such as Sumit Ganguly and Brahma Chellaney, applying the nuclear deterrence logic of Kenneth Waltz, assert that the perceived presence of a secure nuclear second strike capability did deter India and Pakistan from engaging in martial conflict.[11] According to this line of reasoning, the 1999 Kargil incident was an exception that proved the rule. Kargil occurred during a period of temporary nuclear weapons use risk when neither side was certain of the other's ability to deliver a retaliatory nuclear strike. This interim period ended by the time of the 2001–2002 Indo-Pakistan crisis, which began with a terrorist attack on the Indian Parliament by a Pakistan-based Islamic radical group in December 2001.[12]

Quantitative analysis generated by S. Paul Kapur and others from mid-2000s research demonstrated that while some aspects of the optimist position have merit, the specific characteristics of the Indo-Pakistan rivalry display a positive correlation between the growth of antagonist nuclear arsenals and crisis instability. More incidents of military conflict and more months of conflict occurred between India and Pakistan in the period of nuclear weapons development and testing (1990–2002) than in any other time since their independence from Britain in 1947.[13] The majority of these incidents came in the form of insurgent-driven clashes in Jammu-Kashmir or terrorist strikes deep within India. While this pattern does not indicate that the presence of nuclear weapons caused an increase in armed conflict, its clarity indicates that the most prevalent form of subconventional violence perpetrated against India (and, in New Delhi's view, emanating from Pakistan) since at least 1990 makes Pakistani negation of Indian conventional military advantage a paramount enabler of the irregular insurgent or terrorist-initiated strikes at Indian interests. The degree to which Rawalpindi can threaten a credible nuclear strike that deters India from use of its great and growing conventional military advantage against Pakistan in the event of an irregular militia attack against Indian interests is the degree to which Pakistan can stand back from Indian demands that it more effectively throttle what India perceives to be the wellspring of Islamist terrorism on the Subcontinent.

The classic models of enhanced stability through nuclear deterrence that developed during the period of U.S.-Soviet cold war nuclear competition are problematic in application to South Asia. These models depend on a framework where a unitary state actor operates on both sides of the deterrence equation. But the primary dynamic in which conflict between Pakistan and India might escalate into conventional or nuclear war, through escalation from a subconventional (terrorist or extremist militia) clash, involves actors that do not respond, at least at some level, to the strategic direction of the Pakistani state. The challenge of constraining subconventional violent actors capable of sparking the escalation toward nuclear war is a unique and critical variable unaccounted for in historic approaches to deterrence.[14] It reinforces longstanding pessimist worries about the correlation between more nuclear weapons and reduced crisis stability on the Subcontinent. It also mirrors the general resistance of terrorists and other nonstate actors to deterrence as generally understood.

From 1998 to 2006 the size and focus of Indian and Pakistani nuclear weapons programs approached parity. This condition seemed to reinforce, if not actually create, a reasonable degree of crisis stability at the levels of conventional and nuclear war. India chose a nuclear posture featuring "existential deterrence"—declaring a "no first use" policy. New Delhi never developed a doctrine for how nuclear weapons would actually be used in a conflict, short of in retaliation for use of nuclear weapons against its territory. Given that its nuclear arsenal featured relatively large payload weapons for delivery by manned aircraft or land-based missiles, India's lack of nuclear use doctrine led most observers to conclude that New Delhi meant what it said: it would only seek to use nuclear weapons in a retaliatory mode.[15] Pakistan's nuclear policy was deliberately ambiguous, never ruling out first use against India, but with limited prospects for credible nuclear warfighting due to large warhead size and serious questions about the reliability and accuracy of its nuclear delivery systems—including land-based missiles and air-to-surface platforms.[16]

Yet India's tolerance for this stasis was never certain, and it waned after the 2001–2002 crisis. In early 2002 India exercised strategic restraint and eschewed a conventional military response to what it perceived as a Pakistani-sponsored terrorist attack on its parliament. This restraint derived as much from inadequate Indian military capability as from any political decision in New Delhi.[17] Indian military frustration over the existing cumbersome method for conventional military mobilization during this period of the 2001–2002 "Twin Peaks Crisis" led to development of a new conventional warfighting doctrine: "Cold Start."

In theory, Cold Start would enable a critical mass of conventional Indian forces to strike Pakistan in a punitive manner within 48 hours in the event of further irregular militia or terrorist provocation.[18] Announced by the Indian Army in 2004—although never formally endorsed by India's civilian defense leadership—Cold Start remains in 2013 an aspiration rather than a reality. But its impact on Pakistan's defense psyche has been profound.[19] Viewing Cold Start as a means of limited war designed to negate Islamabad's nuclear retaliation capability—either by a decapitating conventional strike or a large and swift incursion into Pakistan rendering a large-scale nuclear response disproportionate—Pakistan began looking for ways to reshape its nuclear arsenal to be a more effective deterrent by making it a more useful option early in an armed clash with India.[20]

Pakistani incentives to make this adjustment only grew stronger in 2006 when the basic framework for a U.S.-India civil nuclear power deal was settled (and ratified in 2008).[21] To Pakistan this agreement gave India unacceptable potential for a massive acceleration in future nuclear weapons material production. Rawalpindi viewed the agreement as a dangerous threat to Pakistan's long-term nuclear deterrent, reducing the credibility of Pakistani nuclear retaliation to a conventional Indian attack and thereby increasing the risk of an Indian conventional strike in response to any future irregular military clashes. Pakistan's nuclear approach needed to adapt, and it did in the mid-2000s.[22]

The consequences of this evolution in Pakistan's approach to its nuclear arsenal are critical to understanding the growing degree of crisis instability on the Subcontinent. From the mid-2000s, Pakistan's nuclear development activity featured growing amounts of nuclear fissile material, especially plutonium-based material. This growth provides Pakistan the resources to make nuclear weapons that are smaller, more accurate, and more usable on the battlefield where Indian military formations might be targeted in response to a conventional attack.[23]

To be fair, Pakistan did balance its activities to enhance the usability of nuclear weapons with others that improved the safety and security of its standing arsenal. From at least 2002, Pakistan's Strategic Plans Division (SPD) worked with the United States to improve safeguards of its existing nuclear forces against accidental or uncontrolled launch. In 2006, the SPD director, retired Pakistani Lieutenant General Khalid Kidwai, reported that these efforts had resulted in comprehensive weapons stockpile safeguards including institution of a two-man rule and establishment of mechanical restraints to prevent accidental or unauthorized use (Permissive Action Links). These, Kidwai declared, provided additional security for Pakistan's nuclear weapons that were already believed to be stored disassembled and separate from delivery vehicles in dispersed locations.[24]

Pakistan's decision to accelerate its nuclear weapons program derived from several factors. The Indian army's announcement of a move toward Cold Start heightened Pakistan's desire for an improved nuclear weapons arsenal as did Pakistani perceptions that the U.S.-Indian civilian nuclear power agreement discriminated against Pakistan and increased India's future ability to process weapons-grade uranium and plutonium despite New Delhi's assurances to the contrary. Finally, Pakistan's military-intelligence complex was increasingly aware of the great and growing Indian conventional military modernization effort—one the Pakistanis feared that, in combination with a Cold Start doctrine and a dramatic increase in weapons grade fissile material, could give India the ability to dominate conflict escalation in most conceivable military contests between the two countries. Any serious Islamist militant attack against Indian interests might lead to a rapid and powerful Indian conventional military reaction that, coupled with India's nuclear deterrent, would neutralize Pakistan's own nuclear deterrent.

Thus, Pakistan's nuclear weapons arsenal has grown dramatically from 2006, and the future arsenal's capabilities have become ever more oriented toward assured survival and short-range, accurate use in a battlefield warfighting scenario. Beginning in 2006, independent reports identified Pakistan as actively looking to purchase advanced nuclear weapons components.[25]

As recently as 2008, observers reported that Pakistan possessed 60–85 nuclear weapons (see table 1),[26] roughly equivalent to the 60–80 operational weapons estimated for India.[27] These numbers derived from calculations that reported Pakistan as having around 2,000 kilograms (kg) of highly enriched uranium and 90 kg of separated military plutonium, enough to make 80–130 implosion-type warheads, but without sufficient delivery vehicles to support a conclusion that all

Table 1. Pakistan's Nuclear Warhead Growth, 1998–2011									
Year	1998	2000	2002	2004	2006	2008	2009	2010	2011
Number of weapons	10–20	20–30	35–50	50–60	60–70	60–85	70–95	80–100	90–110

the fissile material had been made into weapons.[28] From 1999, Pakistan has explained that it only seeks "credible minimal deterrence" from its nuclear arsenal, and that this would be determined independent of what India chose to develop for its forces.[29]

By early 2009, the extent of Pakistan's effort to increase and enhance its nuclear forces was clear. Pakistan began a more focused effort on the elements necessary for plutonium-based warhead designs.[30] Simultaneously, it accelerated expansion of the capacity to produce plutonium at new nuclear power sites.[31] Lighter plutonium warheads would allow for more accurate long-range delivery. More important, smaller plutonium warheads would give Pakistan a battlefield tactical capability via delivery in artillery shells, short range surface-to-surface missiles, and cruise missiles.[32]

Looking at the work begun in 2006 with Chinese assistance on additional heavy water nuclear reactors at the Khushab nuclear power complex (numbers III visible then and IV to follow), nuclear weapons experts at the Federation of Atomic Scientists forecast that the reactors would triple Pakistan's annual plutonium production capacity by 2016. Around the same time, construction of a new plutonium reprocessing facility began at the Pakistan Institute of Nuclear Science and Technology near Rawalpindi.[33] Pakistan also began developing and expanding reprocessing facilities at an expanded Khushab site and two other locations. Plutonium production at the new Khushab II nuclear reactor started in early 2010, and it reportedly first produced plutonium in 2011.[34] Khushab III plutonium production was anticipated as early as 2013, and international observers reported that construction work began on a fourth reactor (Khushab IV) in early 2011. As of late 2010, Pakistan's collective efforts increased its available weapons-grade plutonium to some 100–130 kg, up from 90 kg in 2008.[35] Together, Khushab I and II can generate some 22 kg of plutonium a year, enough for four weapons per annum.[36] When the other two Khushab reactors come on line, Pakistan will be able to more than double its weapons-grade plutonium production for nuclear weapons at a site that is not subject to International Atomic Energy Agency (IAEA) inspection.[37]

Alone, these fissile material developments raise concerns about a fissile nuclear materials race on the Subcontinent.[38] Combined with parallel developments in Pakistan's short-range warhead delivery capability, fissile material production increases already high concerns about crisis stability between Pakistan and India.

Between 2006 and 2009, Pakistan successfully developed and tested medium-range, ground-based nuclear delivery missiles such as the Shaheen-1 and Shaheen-2. Concurrently, it began work on improved short-range ballistic and cruise missiles capable of delivering nuclear warheads. The ground-launched cruise missile Babur (Hatf-7) with a range of 600 kilometers (km) and air-launched cruise missile Ra'ad (Hatf-8) with a 350 km range were the focus of military delivery system development in 2009. Accelerated testing of these cruise missiles continued from 2009 through mid-2012, with full performance capability confirmed during the 2012 tests. Work on a truly short-range, ground-based nuclear-capable missile, the Nasr (Hatf-9), with a 60-km range, also accelerated during the period, with two mostly successful tests of this tactically focused surface-to-surface missile between spring 2011 and spring 2012.[39]

Armed with functioning delivery systems capable of attacking battlefield targets, SPD Director General Kidwai declared in May 2012 that Pakistan's nuclear force had consolidated its deterrence capability at all levels of the threat spectrum, thereby assuring peace in the region.[40] Although subsequent technical issues with the Nasr short-range missile made Kidwai's claim that it was fully operational premature by at least a year, his overall point about Pakistan's greatly enhanced short-range nuclear weapons options was sound.[41] By mid-2012, Islamabad's half-decade focus on development of nuclear-capable short-range and cruise missiles had doubled its number of nuclear missile warhead delivery systems from four to eight, with three of the four newest delivery systems capable of operating in short ranges necessary for tactical battlefield delivery (see table 2).[42]

Table 2. Pakistan's Mid- and Short-range Nuclear Weapons Delivery Systems			
Aircraft	**MRBMs**	**SRBMs**	**Cruise missiles**
F16 A/B (1998) 1,600 km	Ghuari (2003) 1,200+ km	Shaheen-1 (2003) 450+ km	Babur (2011) 600 km
Mirage Vs (1998) 2,100 km	Shaheen-2 (2011) 2,000+ km	Ghaznavi (2004) 400 km	Ra'ad (2012) 350+ km
		Abdali (2012) 180 km	
		Nasr (2014) 60 km	

Key: km = kilometer; MRBMs = mid-range ballistic missiles; SRBMs = short-range ballistic missiles

Pakistan's Past, Present, and Projected Nuclear Weapons Arsenal (to 2020)

DUE TO COPYRIGHT RESTRICTIONS
SOME OR ALL IMAGES ARE NOT INCLUDED

Source: Figure adapted with author's permission from original work by Hans Kristensen, "Nuclear Weapons, Pakistan," *Federation of Atomic Scientists Strategic Security Blog,* July 17, 2011, available at <www.fas.org/programs/ssp/nukes/images/PakistanChart2011.jpg>.

By early 2011, experts pegged Pakistan's nuclear arsenal as in excess of 100 deployed weapons with another 30 feasible due to weapons-grade nuclear material then on hand.[43] This gave Pakistan the sixth largest deployed nuclear arsenal and fifth largest potential nuclear arsenal, behind only the United States, Russia, China, and the United Kingdom. It also produced a Pakistani arsenal that had moved beyond the relative nuclear parity with India that had existed for more than a decade. Given that Pakistan has the know-how for building lighter, smaller tactical nuclear weapons (miniaturization), and for marrying them to battlefield-style delivery systems, it may be able to produce up to 15 tactical nuclear systems a year now and up to 30–35 per year within a decade.[44]

Western security analysts do not all agree on the purpose of Pakistan's focus on smaller nuclear warheads with greater accuracy and shorter delivery ranges. One school of thought contends that the nuclear developments are part of a Pakistani military signaling project aimed at deterring an Indian conventional invasion and galvanizing U.S. and Western attention toward

Islamabad's perceived vulnerabilities and are not aimed at the actual initiation of a limited nuclear war.[45] Others have drawn the opposite conclusion. Citing the need for any credible threat to require a fully thought-out tactical nuclear weapons doctrine and rehearsals, these analysts worry that Pakistan's military is aiming to acquire a tactical use capability in order to launch small, accurate nuclear weapons[46] against massed Indian conventional forces either invading Pakistan or poised for attack.[47]

While it is hard to disentangle a Pakistani tactical nuclear capability robust enough to signal India of its intent to fight a limited nuclear war in response to an Indian conventional incursion from one the Pakistani military can actually use that way, indications now exist that Islamabad has decided to acquire the capability and credible posture for such a tactical nuclear strike. First, SPD officials have stated that Pakistan's nuclear weapons program objectives are not reliant on India's nuclear or conventional buildup, but that it has specific endstate objectives aimed at a finite capability these officials will not divulge.[48] While far from certain, it seems likely that Pakistan's military believes that a tactical arsenal, dispersed for survivability against Indian preemption and capable of striking a tactical nuclear blow against any of the nine Indian division-sized integrated battle groups of armor, aviation, and artillery featured in the evolving Cold Strike doctrine, would be sufficient—independent of Indian nuclear developments—to credibly deter or punish an Indian conventional attack.[49] Second, Pakistan's post-2009 nuclear warhead development and testing activities have focused to a large degree on the accuracy and survivability of small plutonium-based warheads.[50] In this technical and tactical escalation of its nuclear posture, Pakistan aims to threaten the first use of nuclear weapons on Indian ground forces—to include on Pakistani soil—in order to deter significant Indian conventional action.[51] Keen observers of the Pakistani nuclear program also report that Pakistan's development and testing of small warhead, battlefield nuclear weapons is far ahead of any thoughtful contemplation of the risks of battlefield use, greatly increasing the prospects for ill-considered and dangerous use.[52]

On the other side of the dominant South Asian security dilemma, India's pursuit of military capability since 2006 has focused mainly on conventional forces, not nuclear armaments.[53] Although they are dwarfed by conventional modernization efforts, India has continued to improve its nuclear weapons delivery capabilities. The military has focused on developing a nuclear weapons delivery triad, improving the variety and survivability of its land-based missile systems, and adding indigenous ship and submarine delivery capabilities to its well-established air fleet delivery systems.

For almost two decades India fielded a modest number of Russian-made, nuclear-armed, ship-based and submarine-based cruise missiles. Ship-based variants have been on Indian frigates and aboard six Russian-made *Kilo*-class submarines (known as the *Sindhughosh*-class in the Indian navy). These have been limited in range and accuracy and deemed unacceptable by the military as a sea-based component of its nuclear arsenal. An indigenous Indian ship-to-surface missile, the Prithvi-III, has been in the inventory since the early 2000s, but its liquid-reliant propellant requirement has limited its deployability due to the requirements to store liquid fuel in separate bulky containers and fill the rocket just before launch. As a consequence, India's indigenous shipbuilding programs have focused on future deployments of nuclear-powered surface ships and submarines capable of advanced nuclear ordnance launch. India's *Arihant*-class of nuclear-powered ballistic missile submarines began sea testing in 2009. The first *Arihant* submarine planned for full induction into service is to be commissioned in 2013. Up to eight *Arihant*s could be fielded by 2025 and will be equipped with Sagarika nuclear submarine-launched ballistic missiles with a maximum range of 700 km and a 1,000 kg payload.[54] India's development plans for frigates, destroyers, and aircraft carriers will enable incorporation of the nuclear-capable Bramhos cruise missiles, with a range of 290 km, and the Nirbhay, with a range of 1,000 km.

Indian land-delivery efforts have focused on indigenous development and longer ranges and greater accuracy in nuclear payloads. Its Prithvi-I ground-based ballistic missile has been in service since 1994 with a range of 150 km, a payload of 1,000 kg, and limited accuracy. Beginning in 2010, India's Strategic Force Command, along with its air force and army, has tested a long-range, highly accurate nuclear-capable ground-launched missile, the Prithvi-II.[55]

Given these developments, Pakistani fears about the massive expansion potential of Indian nuclear forces may be overstated but not unreasonable. In February 2011 the Federation of American Scientists estimated that India had a stockpile of 80–100 nuclear weapons. That same year a former Indian intelligence official claimed that India was capable of producing 130 kg of weapons-grade plutonium a year from six reactors not included in the safeguarding element of the U.S.-India civil nuclear power deal. In 2012 two American nuclear scientists reported that India actually had a stockpile of 520 kg of weapons-grade plutonium but had not converted it into weapons. They also stated that the construction of a second Indian plutonium-producing reactor at Vishakapatnam and the recent commissioning of a fast breeder reactor near Kalpakkam would greatly enhance weapons-grade plutonium production. Despite these steps, which appear modest in relation to the investment in conventional military modernization, India's nuclear weapons advancements have kept Pakistan's deep fears for its nuclear deterrent alive and abetted Pakistan's rationale for its own nuclear weapons program over the past half-decade.[56]

India's pursuit of antiballistic missile (ABM) technology has been less vigorous than its pursuit of nuclear delivery systems and far shy of its conventional weapons procurement activities.

Active since 1999, the ABM program has developed a modest capability centered on a high altitude interceptor (the Prithvi Air Defense missile) and a low altitude interceptor (the Advance Air Defense missile). These interceptors are integrated with a pair of radar systems based on Israeli designs and acquired by India over the past decade.[57] Small in scale, the Indian ABM program does not threaten the nuclear missile deterrent of either Pakistan or China. As a result, the missile-antimissile dynamic that spurred the Soviet-American nuclear arms race during the Cold War is not present on the Subcontinent. Absent a more dramatic stimulus from other players or dramatically more capable systems in the nuclear missile arena, a nuclear arms race appears unlikely.

In short there are firm grounds for outside observers to worry about the future of crisis stability in South Asia. The preconditions for a classic nuclear arms race are not evident and are unlikely to develop without a choice by India to pursue ballistic missile defense systems.[58] Nonetheless, an asymmetric arms race is well underway. It features Pakistan focusing on its battlefield nuclear arsenal and India pursuing short-term conventional weapons advancements and a robust nuclear weapons triad for the future. Public rhetoric by India's military regarding its Cold Start conventional capability to attack Pakistan in the event of another major terrorist or Islamist militia strike does not match India's actual military capabilities, but it does heighten Islamabad's angst and drive its nuclear weapons security choices in a highly destabilizing direction.

Pakistan's development of battlefield nuclear weapons capability is advancing well ahead of any serious analysis of the risks from dispersion of nuclear weapons on the battlefield or the escalatory consequences from use of battlefield nuclear arms.[59] These bilateral security dynamics drive an ever-growing risk that nuclear weapons might be used inadvertently or as a result of a spiral of escalation from a subconventional altercation and a product of unintended consequences from the tense security dilemma on the Subcontinent.

At the same time, a separate nuclear weapons development in the region does have the potential to affect the future of nuclear arms race stability on the Subcontinent. Iran's nuclear program merits discussion in terms of crisis and arms race stability implications for Pakistan and India.

Iran's Nuclear Program: A Variable without Direct Impact on Crisis and Arms Race Stability on the Subcontinent

Although Iran professes to have no nuclear weapons program and that such a program would be inconsistent with its ideology, many nuclear experts believe along with the IAEA that Iran has since at least 2003 run its nuclear program in a manner so that it will have the option to build a bomb in a short period of time should it make the political decision to do so.[60] The program seems to be inspired by several motivations. The first is regime survival. The clerical leadership is believed to have determined that possession of a nuclear weapon might best deter American intervention or invasion aimed at causing regime change, as occurred in Iraq and Libya.[61] It is also motivated by national, ethnic, and religious pride. Persian Shi'ite Iran believes it is culturally and technologically capable of a nuclear weapon achievement and aims to enhance civic pride just as the 1998 nuclear weapons test by Pakistan generated enormous civic pride in that Sunni Muslim state.[62]

Iran's nuclear program is not aimed at either Pakistan or India.[63] There is no evidence that Tehran has ever felt a physical threat from Pakistan—before or since Pakistan's 1998 acquisition of nuclear weapons. Relations between the two countries—very warm during the 1950s through the 1970s and then tense in the years immediately after the coup by Ayatollah Khomeini in Iran—have been largely stable and respectful since the mid-1980s.[64] The shared Persian-Pakistani border astride respective Baluchistan regions has witnessed episodic violence and complaints of insurrectionist leaders operating from cross-border locations. Successful diplomacy ensured that these tensions have not threatened regional peace.

India's interactions with Iran are shaped by trade and commerce (especially raw material exports from Iran to India), the cultural interaction of India's 16 to 24 million Shi'a Muslims, and limited military-to-military relations.[65] Despite few formal relations with foreign militaries, Iran and India have a "strategic dialogue," and a few officers from Iran's navy have been trained in India.[66] New Delhi's interests in Iran have underwritten a cordial, if complicated, relationship.

Any Iranian nuclear weapons ambitions thus would not focus on Pakistan or India in a direct way. However, Iran's longest range ballistic missile that could be used to deliver a nuclear payload at some point in the future, the *Shahab-3*, can range both Islamabad and New Delhi as well as Kuwait City, Doha, Dubai, and Riyadh.[67]

Therefore, it is unsurprising that both countries, while defending Iran's right to nuclear power, prefer that Iran acquire no nuclear weapons. Pakistan's military has remained mute, but its political leaders have publicly urged Iran against building nuclear weapons. In 2006 Foreign Minister Khurshid Kasuri stated, "We are the only Muslim country [with nuclear weaponry], and don't want anyone else to get it."[68] Similarly, Foreign Minister Mehmood Qureshi answered a question during a 2010 visit to Harvard University about Iran's nuclear program by declaring, "In my view, I don't think they have a justification to go nuclear. They have an international obligation. They have signed [the Nuclear Nonproliferation Treaty] and they should respect that."[69]

Contrasting Iran with Pakistan, Qureshi noted that Islamabad faced a severe security threat from a neighboring nuclear state, India, and that he saw no similar immediate threat to Iran.[70] Qureshi's public remarks aligned with those from Former Pakistani Prime Minister Yousuf Raza Gilani's June 2010 pronouncement that Pakistan would support United Nations–mandated sanctions against Iran for its nuclear program but would not feel compelled to back unilateral U.S. sanctions against Tehran.[71]

Concerned with bilateral economic engagement and with maintaining calm within India's extensive Shi'ite Muslim minority community, New Delhi's political leadership has subtly but consistently expressed its nuclear preferences for Iran. Although slow to join in international economic and diplomatic sanctions against Iran, Prime Minister Manmohan Singh has stated clearly since 2005 that India, "doesn't wish Iran to be a nuclear state."[72] These sentiments were restated in detail by Singh's Foreign Secretary Ranjan Mathai in the summer of 2012:

> *Peace and security is indeed our primary concern given just how important the entire West Asian region and the Gulf region in particular are for India's security, for the very large number of Indian citizens who live in that region and for the Indian economy both in terms of our oil imports and our exports. So, this is our own concern and we do not have to take anybody else's concern as being a priority over that. This is indeed our own very specific concern.*[73]

Thus, while neither New Delhi nor Islamabad has been proactive in working to inhibit Tehran's acquisition of nuclear weapons, neither desires that Iran become a nuclear weapons state.

While a demonstrable direct threat to the Subcontinent is not evident, Iran's attainment of a credible nuclear weapons arsenal will have an indirect impact on the future of nuclear arms race stability between Pakistan and India. This impact will arise through an Arabian connection, which will be analyzed in the following section. The timing and degree of Iran's nuclear program impact on arms race stability on the Subcontinent will have much to do with the ultimate status of Iran's nuclear program. In this context, there are three main possibilities for the program:

The first possibility is that Iran becomes a virtual nuclear weapons state that moves to a "break-out capability" in its nuclear program but does not declare or test its nuclear arsenal. The second is that Iran becomes a declared but untested nuclear weapons state—one that declares its acquisition of a nuclear weapons capability, but without a formal test of a nuclear device. The third is that Iran formally becomes a nuclear weapons state that has both declared itself to have nuclear weapons and has completed a successful test of its nuclear bomb.

If Iran advances no further than a virtual a nuclear weapons state, then its nuclear program is unlikely to have much effect on arms race or crisis stability between Pakistan and India. However, advancement to either a "declared but untested" or a "formal" nuclear state would almost certainly have implications for Saudi Arabia, Pakistan, and India, and thus indirectly have an impact on the status of nuclear proliferation and crisis stability on the Subcontinent.

To become a virtual nuclear weapons power, Iran would be required to reach and maintain a nuclear-weapons "break-out capacity." Here, Iran would achieve the capacity to manufacture nuclear weapons within 12 to 15 months and possess the delivery systems to use them, but would stop short of actually bringing these components together. By not declaring its program or testing its weapons designs, Tehran might achieve standing as a nuclear weapons–capable state, achieving some measure of deterrence against American attack without deliberately flaunting the international system with a declaration or a test.[74] Unclassified reports indicate that the classified 2010 U.S. National Intelligence Estimate was the product of considerable debate within the U.S. Government regarding the trajectory of Iran's nuclear program and suggests that Iran's leaders may want to avoid the international condemnation and military reprisals that could result from a declared nuclear capability.[75]

Current social unrest across the Middle East and within Iran may make Tehran even less willing to risk the economic and security consequences of overt nuclearization. By not actually building a bomb, Iran could maintain its stated policy against nuclear weapons on religious grounds and status as a member of the Treaty on the Non-Proliferation of Nuclear Weapons (NPT). Threats to withdraw from the NPT unless its security or economic needs are addressed might be a sign that Iran has attained "break-out capabilities."[76] As Middle East and South Asia security expert Bruce Reidel observed during 2011, if Iran simply acquires the capability and begins to build a nuclear arsenal without public acknowledgement or a test, the security impacts will be tectonic rather than volcanic.[77]

A decision to cross the nuclear threshold, secretly manufacture a nuclear weapon, and then openly declare its status while refraining from testing a weapon is another possibility. While it is unlikely that an undeclared nuclear capacity is Tehran's desired endstate, it could choose this outcome. This course would open Iran to most of the negative consequences of nuclearization without the full advantages of becoming a nuclear-armed state. Iran could use its nuclear weapons covertly or through proxies (such as terrorist groups), but with knowledge that it could expect nuclear or massive conventional retaliation for attacks that were traced back to Iranian sources. Meanwhile, the lack of a tested nuclear capability would limit the value of nuclear weapons in improving Iran's status as a regional and global power—clearly an important issue to Iran's leaders. Further, if Iran's pursuit of nuclear weapons is motivated in part by the desire to end Western intervention in the Middle East and Persian Gulf region, an undeclared nuclear capability might be less effective at dissuading Western states from military engagement there.[78] Declaration of a nuclear weapons capability would risk greater damage to Iran's important economic relations with India. Furthermore, mere declaration of a nuclear weapons capability is likely to prompt Saudi Arabia and other Arab countries such as the United Arab Emirates (UAE), Qatar, and Kuwait to obtain nuclear weapons themselves.[79]

Finally, Iran could become an official nuclear weapons state by building and testing a nuclear weapon. This is a more likely scenario than the development of ambiguous nuclear capabilities but would require a major government commitment to weather the full weight of negative consequences of nuclearization. These would likely include even more draconian economic sanctions and the possibility of military attack by Israel, the United States, or even the North Atlantic Treaty Organization.[80] While nuclear status would increase Iran's prestige and contribute to its national self-image as a regional power, it might come at economic and political costs its leaders are not willing to bear, particularly as the regime contends with social unrest and an economy already crippled by sanctions. Moreover, such an ultimate posture for Iran's nuclear program seems certain to excite Saudi Arabia to acquire nuclear weapons with both a long- and short-term approach. As with the declared but untested scenario, response maneuvering by Riyadh would almost certainly involve Pakistan.[81]

Saudi Arabia's Response to Iran's Nuclear Decisions: A Variable with Indirect Impact on Arms Race Stability on the Subcontinent

Other than Israel, Saudi Arabia views itself as having the most to lose from Iranian acquisition of a nuclear weapon. Saudi worries nest within wider concerns about what is viewed as Tehran's strategic aim of intimidating and neutralizing Sunni Muslim states while championing Shia Muslim minority rights across the greater Middle East.[82]

Consistent with a historically unfriendly relationship, tolerable coexistence turned to extreme tensions between Riyadh and Tehran after the 1979 ascension to power in Iran of Shi'ite Muslim leader Ayatollah Khomeini. Sunni Muslims viewed Khomeini's brand of assertive Shi'ite Islam governance and regional aspirations as provocative. Being in a stronger fiscal and diplomatic position to react than many of its Sunni Arab neighbors, the House of Saud led Sunni Muslim efforts to blunt the regional impact of Khomeini's Shi'ite revolution. A major component of this effort to check Persian-led Shi'ite ascendance played out in quiet but significant Saudi support for Iraqi leader Saddam Hussein's war against Iran, begun by Saddam in late 1980 and active through 1988.[83] For another decade and a half, Saudi Arabia continued to rely upon Saddam's Iraq as the front-line agent check to Iranian ambitions.

This relationship was undone by the American-led 2003 military campaign to topple Saddam's regime and the ensuing remake of electoral politics in a manner that saw an Iraqi Shia, Nouri al-Maliki, become prime minister. From Riyadh's perspective, the deeply unsettling political makeover in Iraq was the product of American naïveté and generated a "win" for Iran's dangerous ambition of extending a regional Shi'ite crescent. Riyadh's worries over Tehran's regional gains grew more acute with the 2010 U.S. failure to conclude a strategic forces arrangement with Iraq, securing a long-term American military presence there. The Saudis viewed the late 2011 departure of all American forces from Iraq as the end of a limited but meaningful American presence capable of deterring worrisome Iranian collusion with Iraqi Shi'ite leaders.[84]

The Saudis have heard American leaders talk about "extended nuclear deterrence" for the Arabian Peninsula—presumably against Iran.[85] However, Riyadh harbors enormous doubts about American reliability.[86] Therefore, the Saudis (and the United Arab Emirates and Qatar) took steps from 2006 to 2011 to generate a civilian nuclear power capability and signal Riyadh's willingness to explore all its options toward acquisition of an independent nuclear weapons deterrent if necessary.[87] Reportedly, Riyadh plans to spend more than $88 billion on 16 nuclear reactors by 2030.[88]

Beginning in 2011, unofficial and off-the-record Saudi spokesmen have hinted far more bluntly than ever before about independent plans to counter Iranian acquisition of a nuclear weapons capability.[89] Between June and November 2011, influential but without official portfolio Saudi Prince Turki al-Faisal made worldwide news by stating that the Kingdom may have no choice but to arm itself with nuclear weapons to counter an emerging threat from Iran.[90] A February 2012 report by the *Times of London* cited unnamed Saudi officials as determined to match Tehran if it goes nuclear. The officials said that Riyadh would conduct a two-part nuclear response by first purchasing off-the-shelf warheads from abroad with rapid work on a ballistic missile launch platform to provide a rapid autonomous deterrent.[91] Simultaneously, the Saudis would enhance their planned civil nuclear program to allow for weapons-grade uranium development over the long term.[92]

While Saudi Arabia's resolve to acquire nuclear weapons seems unlikely to be triggered if Iran culminates its nuclear program at a "break-out capacity," an Iranian declaration or declaration/test of a nuclear weapon seems almost certain to elicit the signaled Saudi Arabian response.[93] That response would certainly involve Pakistan and potentially China at some level.[94] In turn, that response would have implications for crisis and arms race stability on the Subcontinent.

Saudi Arabia has a long and intertwined history with Pakistan.[95] This history—underpinned by a common Sunni Muslim heritage—has religious, cultural, economic, and political dimensions. It also has military dimensions dating back decades. Pakistani pilots and ground troops have assisted with defense of the Kingdom in separate actions during the 1960s, 1970s, and 1980s.[96] Military-to-military relations remain close. Chief among these military-strategic interactions between the Kingdom and Pakistan has been their relationship in the course of Pakistan's development of nuclear energy and nuclear weapons.[97]

Saudi Arabia's unique relationship with Pakistan during Islamabad's civilian nuclear power and nuclear weapons development program makes this an especially important connection in the event of an ever-widening chain of Middle East and South Asia nuclear weapons proliferation in response to an Iranian nuclear weapon. Should Saudi Arabia determine it to be politically necessary to acquire nuclear weapons as a deterrent to Iran, Pakistan would be its most likely accomplice. China and Saudi Arabia have underwritten Pakistan's development of nuclear power and acquisition of nuclear weapons. While the Chinese have provided the bulk of the technology and nuclear power generation know-how, Saudi Arabia has financed much of Pakistan's nuclear weapons program.[98] Saudi money also cushioned Pakistan against the impact of western sanctions after Islamabad conducted its first nuclear test in 1998.[99]

Although officially denied in Riyadh and Islamabad, many experts believe that a secret and long-standing agreement exists that Pakistan would provide the Kingdom with nuclear technology and weapons should the Saudis feel threatened by a third party nuclear program. Observers of this relationship believe that the agreement was most recently re-signed in October 2003 when then–Crown Prince Abdullah made a state visit to Islamabad. Pakistani President Asif Ali Zardari has reportedly verbally reaffirmed the Pakistani promise on his state visits to the Kingdom since 2008. Mid-2012 press reports suggest that Pakistani Prime Minister Raja Ashraf took the occasion of a summer visit to Saudi Arabia to meet with King Abdullah in Jeddah to validate the long-standing deal and confirm the details of preliminary coordination such as training Saudi special forces in Pakistan for the rigors of safeguarding nuclear weapons.[100]

Should such an arrangement exist, there are ample possibilities for the deployment—most likely temporary, but potentially permanent—of Pakistani nuclear weapons in a deterrent posture for the Kingdom from their current locations in South Asia, or by direct introduction into the Kingdom itself. The first possibility is for Saudi Arabia to ask Pakistan for a declaration that its nuclear weapons would be made available from sites in Pakistan in retaliation for any use of nuclear weapons against the Kingdom by Iran.

A more direct possibility is for Pakistan to commit some of its nuclear armed airplanes and pilots into Saudi airfields. Pakistan's air force often trains and exercises with Saudi pilots, and there are many commonalities in command and control approaches.[101] Pakistan might also send nuclear-capable missiles and trained crews to Saudi Arabia. That would take more time and require Saudi spending on launch-capable pads, nuclear storage facilities, and control systems that do not currently exist in the Kingdom.[102] Each of these options has the additional advantage of aligning with the interpretation of the NPT that enabled American stationing of its nuclear weapons in Europe during the Cold War, namely that if nuclear weapons material remained under at least shared Pakistani control in peacetime, the Saudis would effectively join the nuclear club without technical violation of the NPT.[103]

Alternatively, Pakistan might be asked to commence transfer of the technical know-how and capacity for nuclear weapons into Saudi Arabia in a phased process. This approach, if not combined with one of the above conditions, would take considerable time and be of significant concern to Saudi Arabia's neighbors including Israel.

Despite the growing vigor in unofficial Saudi proclamations regarding its intent to respond to a nuclear Iran, it is impossible to know precisely which approach the Kingdom's leadership would pursue should Iran declare itself a nuclear power with or without a successful nuclear test. It is clear as of early 2013, however, that the Saudi leadership mistrusts American leadership—and American promises—more than at any time in the recent history of U.S.-Saudi relations.[104] Thus, even a firm American declaration of extended nuclear deterrence in support of Riyadh and its Sunni Arab neighbors seems unlikely to be taken as the sole Saudi approach.[105] The Kingdom is likely to seek Pakistan's assistance in some capacity.

As noted above, Pakistan's specific arrangements with Saudi Arabia on the matter of nuclear weapons remain opaque. It is easier to discern the factors that would influence Pakistan's approach to a Saudi request for nuclear assistance. Pakistani military and SPD officials make it clear that they wish to avoid responding to a Saudi request for nuclear weapons assistance, hoping that extended American nuclear deterrence might fill the need.[106] Should Saudi mistrust of American reliability make this view unrealistic, Pakistan seems likely to respond while adhering to four imperatives.

First, Islamabad will minimize provocation of Beijing. China's technical know-how underpins the vast majority of Pakistan's nuclear power capacity and armaments designs.[107] Despite autonomous technological capabilities, Pakistan would require Chinese support to transfer nuclear weapons expertise to Saudi Arabia. This imperative, coupled with Chinese reluctance to be seen as a nuclear weapons supplier, suggests that Pakistan would prefer a short-term transfer of nuclear weapons capability rather than the export of a full nuclear weapons development program in response to a Saudi request. While it is unlikely that China would stand in the way of a more formal nuclear weapons transfer, based on its past willingness to transfer ballistic missiles to Saudi Arabia, Pakistani deference to Chinese sensitivities remains a strong imperative.[108]

Second, Pakistan will attempt to minimize dispersion of, or disruption of, its nuclear deterrent against India. As mentioned earlier, this deterrent is growing exponentially, yet Pakistani military and intelligence officials still believe it is insufficient to counter Indian conventional and nuclear threats to Pakistani sovereignty. This imperative would encourage Pakistan to help Saudi Arabia only with a minimum transfer of nuclear weapons assets or know-how away from the Subcontinent. It will skew Pakistan's preference toward assistance provided in such a way that Riyadh could claim to have its own nuclear retaliatory capability in the short term with very little transfer of nuclear capable delivery systems—presumably airplanes—to the Kingdom itself.

Third, Pakistan would seek to avoid provocation of the United States and the wider international community by abetting the permanent transfer of nuclear weapons know-how to a third party country, especially one that is a signatory to the NPT.[109] Pakistan's political leadership understands the depths to which the A.Q. Khan nuclear weapons assistance program, which benefited Iran, damaged its relationship with the international community. The military is less worried about the fallout from the Khan affair but recognizes the damage that a repeat offense of nuclear know-how transfer could do to it worldwide.[110] This imperative would also encourage Pakistan to respond to Saudi Arabia in a manner that promised rhetorical support and limited transfer of assets but not know-how.

Finally, the military and civilian establishments would take into account Israel's reaction to any nuclear weapons collaboration with Saudi Arabia. Pakistan's nuclear weapons developments have consistently taken Israel into account. Insiders have made outside observers aware that the Pakistani military and nuclear agencies have consciously and consistently limited the ranges of nuclear-capable missiles to be less than ranges required to reach Israel. From at least the time of the Israeli aerial attack of the suspected Iraqi nuclear reactor at Osirak in June 1981, Islamabad's military and nuclear establishment feared that Israel might conduct a similar raid against nuclear facilities (from bases in India or elsewhere) if Tel Aviv believed that Islamabad possessed nuclear weapons delivery means to threaten Israel. Thus, Pakistan took an approach that clearly signaled self-limitation of its nuclear delivery system to ranges well shy of those required to reach Tel Aviv, understanding these to be less provocative regionally and internationally.[111] This continuing imperative would reinforce a Pakistani preference for provision of a nuclear deterrence guarantee for Saudi Arabia with use of assets based in Pakistan that don't threaten to reach Israel.[112] If such an arrangement were unacceptable in Riyadh, Pakistani officials likely would offer assistance to Saudi Arabia with a loaned deterrent of nuclear armed aircraft, for these would be easier for Israel to counter with standard air defense options and would not threaten the new specter of nuclear missiles from Saudi Arabia or an indigenous Saudi program to build its own bomb.

Stability Implications: Regional and Super-regional

On the Subcontinent, the erosion of crisis stability between India and Pakistan is obvious and increasingly exacerbated by their evolving security competition. India's long-term pursuit of a nuclear weapons triad, largely to keep pace with China, and most important, its near-term pursuit of comprehensive conventional weapons modernization and a more capable quick-strike conventional force, have excited Pakistan's fears of a compromised nuclear deterrent and a more certain Indian punitive conventional response to a new terrorist strike on Indian soil. Pakistan's vigorous pursuit of a battlefield nuclear weapons capability coupled with its inability or unwillingness to constrain subconventional Islamist militant groups from attacks against Indian interests has set in place a circumstance where escalation from subconventional to nuclear conflict is more plausible than ever.

Iran's acquisition of a nuclear weapons capability will neither exacerbate nor mitigate the worrisome trajectory of crisis stability between India and Pakistan. However, its choices for its nuclear program will affect nuclear arms race incentives on the Subcontinent. Should Iran choose to move beyond a "break-out capability" and culminate its nuclear program with an announced nuclear weapons capability, test such a capability, or both, Saudi Arabia's almost certain response would be to secure its own nuclear weapons deterrent. Due to its relationship with Pakistan, Saudi acquisition of nuclear weapons could occur in months, not decades.

Confronted with the prospect of a nuclear-armed Saudi Arabia—and the high possibility that other Arab states might then work toward long-term acquisition of nuclear weapons—New Delhi would face a more complicated future for its nuclear deterrent than it has ever contemplated. At the very least, New Delhi's rather tepid pursuit of antiballistic missile systems would be revisited and most likely accelerated. Any such acceleration would excite Pakistani and likely Chinese concerns over the long-term viability of their nuclear deterrents against India. In turn, this would stimulate nuclear arms race incentives in a manner characteristic of the missile-antimissile defense dynamic witnessed between America and the Soviet Union at the height of the Cold War.

India's long-standing reluctance to provoke Chinese concern over its nuclear deterrent would be challenged, and should China respond with more of its own nuclear missiles, the region would embark on an unprecedented nuclear arms race with the potential to approach that undertaken between the United States and the Soviet Union during the Cold War. In this manner, the likely Saudi response to an Iranian nuclear weapons program beyond a "break-out capacity" would spur nuclear proliferation incentives in the Near East to a degree that would complicate nuclear deterrence planning for New Delhi and risk stimulating antiballistic missile programs in at least a three-way arms race involving China, Pakistan, and India.

Implications for U.S. Policy

South Asian crisis stability dynamics—or, more accurately, instability dynamics—are troubling in early 2013. The sixth and seventh largest nuclear-armed countries in the world, both with a history of miscalculation of each other's political and military intentions, are deeply enmeshed in an asymmetric arms race. India seems unwilling to accept that its modernization of conventional military forces for possible use in a reprisal attack against Pakistan in the event of another major subconventional/militant attack is of limited deterrent value to the constellation of subnational actors capable of such a strike. Pakistan appears enamored with the once fashionable but long-since discredited Cold War notion that escalation from tactical nuclear exchange to major nuclear war can be limited. Islamabad and New Delhi also have a history of rejecting outside diplomatic assistance in improving deterrence and reducing the misunderstandings most likely to produce a military clash. In this environment, there is little that an outside power such as the United States can do. Nonetheless, the stakes are high enough that a realistic and concerted effort should be made.

First, the United States must publicly flag the severity of the risk of nuclear war now growing between India and Pakistan. American preoccupation with Afghanistan's internal dynamics and counterterrorism activities in the Afghanistan-Pakistan region have crowded out sober discussion of the nuclear crisis risks now overwhelmingly present on the Subcontinent.[113]

Second, the United States should sponsor open dialogue and communication with Pakistan's military and civilian leadership about the grave risks from tactical nuclear weapons, and be candid about the folly of American Cold War thinking about the prospects for limited nuclear war on an acceptable scale.[114]

Third, the United States should appreciate that the risks of escalation from subconventional to a nuclear exchange between Pakistan and India falls most heavily on places where their proxy forces come in contact, and that Afghanistan is now the chief location for this risky interaction.

As a consequence, proper and sufficient residual American military and diplomatic presence in Afghanistan is important. Washington's role in developing the Afghan National Security Forces (ANSF) has produced a force of more than 300,000 well-trained and capable small unit fighters that could disaggregate into lethal and capable militia proxies for India and Pakistan without the cohesion of international advisors and mentors through at least the end of this decade.

In addition, a sufficient residual force of American and coalition military and diplomatic assets in Afghanistan is postured to back up American warnings against intemperate subconventional or conventional military clashes leading to nuclear exchange. As Thomas Schelling famously argued during the height of the Cold War, "What can 7,000 American troops—or 12,000 Allied troops do [in Berlin]? Bluntly, they can die."[115] The residual presence of 20,000–23,000 American and coalition troops in Afghanistan beyond 2014 serves to advise and cleave the ANSF as well as remind Islamabad and New Delhi of the extra-regional complications should American forces face death from their imprudent escalation to a nuclear exchange.

At the same time, American policy should better appreciate the real possibility of a nuclear weapons capability transfer between Pakistan and Saudi Arabia should Iran formally go nuclear. Washington should have a policy plan to help avert such a transfer and to mitigate the worst outcomes for nuclear stability and security should such a transfer occur.

In the first instance, Washington should continue what it is doing to arrest the Iranian nuclear program short of weapons acquisition. The policies of economic and diplomatic sanctions as well as those of nonlethal disruption of the elements of a successful Iranian nuclear program should continue. Should sanctions and disruption fail, America should prefer that Iran culminate its program at no greater than a "break-out capability" endstate. Then it should work with the Saudis and other Gulf states to accede to this imperfect Iranian strategic choice without resort to outside acquisition of nuclear weapons. In this circumstance, an American promise of extended nuclear deterrence to its Gulf allies and partners might be viewed as acceptable, especially when paired with a continuing American military presence in countries such as Qatar, Bahrain, and Kuwait.[116]

Should Iran take its nuclear program to the point of provoking Saudi Arabia's pursuit of its own nuclear weapons, and an American offer of extended nuclear deterrence is viewed as insufficient in Riyadh, Washington should be prudently postured to minimize the proliferation incentives that will be unleashed in the Middle East and the blowback into South Asia. It will be very difficult for America to deter a Pakistan-Saudi nuclear weapons arrangement through threats of punishment. Instead, Washington should tolerate the least destabilizing of the options available to these longstanding military partners. While firmly opposing Pakistani transfer of nuclear weapons or missile delivery systems know-how or program development capabilities to Saudi Arabia, the American administration should accept the kind of transfer that would be least threatening to Israel, least likely to risk "me-too" nuclear weapons program acquisition by other oil-rich Arab nations, and least likely to generate Indian fears for its nuclear deterrent and accelerated interest in ABM development.

Adhering to these principles, the United States should grudgingly accept the temporary transfer of nuclear weapons deterrence capability from Pakistan to Saudi Arabia—provided from Pakistani locations, Saudi locations, or both. America should prefer that any physical transfer of capability be limited to aircraft delivery systems and be in small numbers. These features would be the least threatening to Israel in both the short and long term, reinforcing a long-standing Pakistani nuclear weapons posture imperative. The minimal attributes of such a transfer would also reduce the potential for Arab states such as Qatar, UAE, or Kuwait to pursue a similar deal, thereby being less provocative regionally, on the Subcontinent, and internationally.[117]

A final policy imperative is to realize that the delicate nature of U.S. efforts to temper the growing stability crisis in South Asia and the limited but important impact of Iranian nuclear weapons decisions on Mideast and South Asian nuclear proliferation incentives requires a prudent assessment of both diplomatic access and military presence. As frustrating and provocative as Pakistan remains to the United States regarding Afghanistan, Islamic terrorist groups, and its robust nuclear weapons program, total isolation of Islamabad could push its elites into a corner from which they see risky behavior against India, or in support of Saudi Arabia versus Iran, as necessary. Much as residual American military and diplomatic presence in Afghanistan is important to hedge against an explosive Indo-Pakistani proxy war, the desirability of continuing American diplomatic and military access to Pakistan is prudent in informing Pakistani crisis management and proliferation decisions in a manner that does the least harm to regional and international stability.

Notes

[1] Pakistan has not acknowledged that it is developing tactical nuclear weapons. However, numerous Western and Indian security analysts are certain that Pakistan's intense pursuit of plutonium-based warheads and nuclear-capable missiles such as the sixty-kilometer (or Hatf-9) missile indicate an unambiguous pursuit of just such a capacity. Several of these experts will be cited later in this paper. Among those the reader might consider at this point in the monograph, two stand out: Michael Krepon, "Pakistan's Tactical Nuclear Weapons," *Spotlight* (Washington, DC: Stimson Center, April 24, 2012), available at <www.stimson.org/spotlight/pakistans-tactical-nuclear-weapons/>; and Aditi Malhotra, "Pakistan's Flirtation with Tactical Nuclear Weapons," *Scholar Warrior* (New Delhi: Centre for Land Warfare Studies, Autumn 2012), 76–81.

[2] For several prominent historic examples among many such writings, see Brahma Chellaney, "South Asia's Passage to Nuclear Power," *International Security* 16, no. 1 (Summer 1991), 43–72; Devin Hagerty, *The Consequences of Nuclear Proliferation: Lessons from South Asia* (Cambridge: MIT Press, 1998); Sumit Ganguly, "India's Pathway to Pokhran II: The Prospects and Sources of New Delhi's Nuclear Weapons Program," and Samina Ahmed, "Pakistan's Nuclear Weapons Program: Turning Points and Nuclear Choices," both in *International Security* 23, no. 4 (Spring 1999), 148–204; Sumit Ganguly and S. Paul Kapur, *India, Pakistan and the Bomb: Debating Nuclear Stability in South Asia* (New York: Columbia University Press, 2010); and Vipin Narang, "Posturing for Peace? Pakistan's Nuclear Postures and South Asia Stability," *International Security* 34, no. 3 (Winter 2009/2010).

[3] For examples, see Rodney Jones, "Nuclear Escalation Ladders in South Asia," a Defense Threat Reduction Agency Advanced Systems and Concepts Office report, ASCO 2011-007, April 2011; Phillip C. Saunders, "Overlapping Security Dilemmas in Asia," unpublished Monterrey Institute of International Studies monograph, 2001.

[4] Iran denies that it has a nuclear weapons program, stating that its nuclear developments are strictly for peaceful purposes. The International Atomic Energy Agency (IAEA), first in its 2007 report on Iran and in detail on its 2011 report on Iran, continues to express grave concern about what it describes as "the possible existence in Iran of past or current undisclosed nuclear related activities involving military related organizations, including activities related to the development of a nuclear payload for a missile." The 2011 report lays out clearly that the lack of Iranian cooperation on the possible military dimensions of its nuclear program make it impossible for the IAEA to verify that Iran's nuclear activities are strictly peaceful in nature. See *Implementation of the NPT Safeguards Agreement and relevant provisions of the Security Council resolutions in the Islamic Republic of Iran* (New York: IAEA Board of Governors, February 25, 2011), 7–8; and David Albright, Andrea Stricker, and Christina Walrond, *IAEA Iran Safeguards Report: Expansion of Natanz Enrichment Plant Lags; LEU Production Not as High as Expected; Iran Readying Advance Centrifuges for Deployment?; Continued Non-Cooperation on Military Dimensions* [Rev. 1] (Washington, DC: Institute for Science and International Security, February 25, 2011), 4. While many independent analysts contend that Iran's activities and cooperative failings mean that it has a nuclear weapons program, this paper acknowledges the remaining doubt about Iran's martial intent with its nuclear activities, refers to "the Iranian nuclear program" in the present, and only addresses future Iranian "possibilities" for moving into a nuclear weapons status.

[5] "First strike" stability and "deterrence" stability are among the multiple dimensions of the wider rubric of "strategic" stability that evolved during the Cold War in the specific context of U.S. and Soviet incentives to initiate a nuclear strike against the other. *Deterrence* stability generally refers to a condition in which a would-be aggressor does not initiate war with nuclear weapons because the anticipated costs outweigh the anticipated gains. *First strike* stability is the absence of pressure or incentives for a nuclear first strike. Perceived advantages in a first strike could lead to instability by creating reciprocal fear of surprise attack and war that neither side desires. For many during the Cold War, the solution to the potential for first strike instability was mutually maintained arsenals that could survive a first strike and deliver a devastating second strike. Today there are intense debates about the degree to which these two concepts provide a useful understanding of "strategic" stability in a post–Cold War world. This paper does not aim to amplify or apply these debates to South Asia, choosing instead to extend the classic formulations of "first strike," "crisis," and "arms race" stability to the contemporary situation in the region. Those with a deeper interest in current debates on strategic stability might consult Elbridge Colby, "Defining Strategic Stability: Reconciling Stability and Deterrence," in *Strategic Stability: Contending Interpretations*, ed. Elbridge A. Colby and Michael S. Gerson, 47–84 (Carlisle, PA: Strategic Studies Institute, U.S. Army War College, January 2013).

[6] These concepts are famously developed in Thomas Schelling, *The Strategy of Conflict* (Cambridge: Harvard University Press, 1960), especially 92–126; and Leon V. Sigal, "Warming to the Freeze," *Foreign Policy*, no. 48 (Fall 1982), 54–65. They are updated in Shane Smith, *The Meaning of Strategic Stability and Implications for U.S.-China Relations*, Research Memo (Washington, DC: Institute of National Strategic Studies, October 15, 2010).

[7] A broad discussion of the optimist and pessimist viewpoints is developed in Scott Sagan, "The Perils of Nuclear Proliferation in South Asia," *Asian Survey* 41, no. 6 (November–December 2001), 1064–1086.

[8] A succinct delineation of these positions is found in contending essays by Scott Sagan and Kenneth Waltz. See Scott D. Sagan, "Nuclear instability in South Asia," in *International Politics: Enduring Concepts and Contemporary Issues*, 6th ed., ed. Robert Art and Robert Jervis, 239–249 (New York: Addison-Wesley, 2003); and Kenneth N. Waltz, "Nuclear Stability in South Asia," in ibid., 250–260.

[9] Political pressure for an unconditional Pakistani military retreat was applied by the United States and on the compromised Pakistani prime minister, Nawaz Sharif. See Strobe Talbott, *Engaging India: Diplomacy, Democracy and the Bomb* (New York: Penguin, 2004), 158–164; and Bruce Riedel, *American Diplomacy and the 1999 Kargil Summit at Blair House*, Center for the Advanced Study of India Policy Paper 17 (Philadelphia: University of Pennsylvania, 2002), available at <http://media.sas. upenn.edu/casi/docs/research/papers/Riedel_2002.pdf>.

[10] For a detailed description of the pessimist position, see S. Paul Kapur in Ganguly and Kapur, *India, Pakistan and the Bomb*, especially 38–45, 50–54, and 74. For its application to the 1999 Kargil War, see Neil Joeck, "The Kargil War and Nuclear Deterrence," in *Nuclear Proliferation in South Asia: Crisis Behaviour and the Bomb*, ed. Sumit Ganguly and S. Paul Kapur, 117–143 (London: Routledge, 2009). Also see an application of that position to the Kargil War and the 2001–2002 "Twin Peaks Crisis" in Dinshaw Mistry, "Tempering Optimism about Nuclear Deterrence in South Asia," *Security Studies* 18, no. 1 (2009), 148–182.

[11] For a description of the optimist position, see Sumit Ganguly in Ganguly and Kapur, especially 37–38, 42–43, and 47–49; and its forerunner in Chellaney, 68–69. For an application of the optimist position to the 1999 Kargil War, see Devin T. Hagerty, "The Kargil War: An Optimistic Assessment," in *Nuclear Proliferation in South Asia*, ed. Ganguly and Kapur, 100–116 (London: Routledge, 2009).

[12] On Kargil, see Timothy Hoyt, "The Buddha Frowns? Tactical Nuclear Weapons in South Asia," in *Tactical Nuclear Weapons: Emergent Threats in an Evolving Security Environment*, ed. Brian Alexander and Alistair Millar, 104 (Washington, DC: Brassey's, Inc., 2003). On the 2001–2002 period, see Polly Nayak and Michael Krepon, *U.S. Crisis Management in South Asia's Twin Peaks Crisis* (Washington, DC: The Stimson Center, 2006).

[13] Even when the 1970s are not included, there is still an upward trend of violence in South Asia. In the nonnuclear period there were 91 months of peace (70.5 percent) and 29 months of dispute (19.7 percent), but only 38 months of peace (29.5 percent) and 118 months of dispute (80.3 percent) in the nuclear period. See Paul Kapur, *Dangerous Deterrent: Nuclear Weapons Proliferation and Conflict in South Asia* (Stanford: Stanford University Press, 2007), 29.

[14] For a detailed discussion of the limitations of the unitary actor model of nuclear deterrence when applied to South Asia, see George Perkovich, *The NonUnitary Model and Deterrence Stability in South Asia* (Washington, DC: The Stimson Center, 2012), especially 6–16. A classic development of the unitary actor model and nuclear weapons is found in Bruce Bueno de Mesquita and William H. Riker, "An Assessment of the Merits of Selective Nuclear Proliferation," *Journal of Conflict Resolution* 26, no. 2 (June 1982), especially 292.

[15] First formally articulated in 2003, India's nuclear doctrine has rested on three pillars initially articulated by noted Indian strategic thinker K. Subrahmanyam in 1999: credible minimum deterrence, civilian command and control, and no first use. See Tanvi Kulkarni and Alankrita Sinha, "Undermining Deterrence? The Non State Actors and India's Nuclear Doctrine," issue brief, Institute of Peace and Conflict Studies (IPCS), 2012, available at <www.ipcs.org/issue-brief/nuclear/undermining-deterrence-the-non-state-actors-and-indias-nuclear-doctrine-196.html>. Subrahmanyam also noted that the Indian no first use approach was informed by an American qualification and that it did not apply to states that might first use biological or chemical weapons against India. See K. Subrahmanyam, "No First Use: An Indian View," *Survival* 51, no. 5 (October/November 2009), 35. Indian National Security Advisor Shri Shivshankar Menon then signaled a shift in the no first use doctrine in October 2010 when he spoke at India's National Defence College (NDC), stating that India's policy was, "No first use against nonnuclear weapon states," declaring that this was in keeping with India's culture of minimal deterrence. See speech by Shri Shivshakar Menon at NDC on "The Role of Force in Strategic Affairs," October 10, 2010, India Ministry of External Affairs Web site, 2012, available at <www.colhariharan.org/2010/10/role-of-force-in-strategic-affairs.html>. For consistency in recent military statements regarding Indian beliefs that nuclear weapons "are not for warfighting," see the report of statements by then–Army Chief General V.K. Singh, in winter 2011, in Hans Christensen, "Indian Army Chief: Nukes Not for Warfighting," Federation of Atomic Scientists (FAS) Strategic Security Blog, January 18, 2011, available at <www.fas.org/blog/ssp/category/pakistan>.

[16] Paul K. Kerr and Mary Beth Nikitin, *Pakistan's Nuclear Weapons: Proliferation and Security Issues*, RL34248 (Washington, DC: Congressional Research Service, June 26, 2012), 12–13.

[17] A detailed review of the 2001–2002 "Twin Peaks" Crisis by researchers Nayak and Krepon also suggests that American diplomatic intervention proved a critical inhibiter to conflict escalation in a pattern they found repeated in many respects during the 2008 Mumbai Crisis. See Nayak and Krepon, *U.S. Crisis Management in South Asia's Twin Peaks Crisis*; and Nayak and Krepon, *The Unfinished Crisis: U.S. Crisis Management After the 2008 Mumbai Attacks* (Washington, DC: The Stimson Center, February 2012).

[18] For a description and analysis of India's Cold Start doctrine, see Walter C. Ladwig III, "A Cold Start for Hot Wars? The Indian Army's New Limited War Doctrine," *International Security* 32, no. 3 (Winter 2007/2008), 158–190; and Nitin Gokhal, "India Military Eyes Combine Threat," *The Diplomat*, January 17, 2012, available at <http://thediplomat.com/2012/01/17/india-military-eyes-combined-threat/>. For more on India's limitations in attaining its doctrinal aims, see Shashank Joshi, "The Mythology of Cold Start," *The New York Times*, November 4, 2011, available at <http://india.blogs.nytimes.com/2011/11/04/the-mythology-of-cold-start/>.

[19] See Feroz Hassan Khan, *Eating Grass: The Making of the Pakistani Bomb* (Stanford: Stanford University Press, 2012), 381–382.

[20] As observed by Indian National Security Advisor Shri Shivshankar Menon in August 2012, India's civilian leadership perceives Pakistan's nuclear weapons program to be aimed at reducing India's conventional military advantage, not for deterrence against nuclear weapons first use: "The possession of nuclear weapons has, empirically speaking, deterred others from attempting nuclear coercion or blackmail against India . . . unlike certain other nuclear weapons states, India's weapons were not meant to redress a military imbalance or some perceived inferiority in conventional terms." Quoted in "India faced N-blackmail thrice: NSA," *Hindustan Times* (India), August 21, 2012.

[21] Pakistani security scholar Ayesha Siddiqa concisely made this point: "The Washington-New Delhi civil nuclear deal is seen [in Pakistan] as disturbing the balance of power in South Asia, which is detrimental to Pakistan's interests." Ayesha Siddiqa, "Pakistan's Counterterrorism Strategy: Separating Friends from Enemies," *The Washington Quarterly*, Winter 2011, 157, available at <http://ancien.operationspaix.net/IMG/pdf/WQ_PakistansCounterterrorismStrategy_SeparatingFriendsFromEnemies_2011-01-03_.pdf>.

[22] Retired Pakistani Brigadier and Nuclear Forces General Feroz Khan refers to this as a period when Pakistan had to confront the gaps in its "minimum deterrence" construct for nuclear weapons and began a qualitative diversification in its forces. See Feroz Hassan Khan, "Minimum Deterrence: Pakistan's Dilemma," *RUSI Journal* 156, no. 5 (October/November 2011), 44–51; and Khan, *Eating Grass*, 380–384.

[23] See Mansoor Ahmed, "Why Pakistan needs tactical nuclear weapons," *The Weekly Pulse*, May 6, 2011, available at <www.weeklypulse.org/details.aspx?contentID=563&storylist=9>. Also see Directorate for Inter Services Public Relations, Press Release on the Test of the Nasr (Hatf-IX) short range ballistic missile: No PR94/2011-ISPR, April 19, 2011, available at <www.ispr.gov.pk/front/main.asp?o=t-press_release&id=1721>.

[24] Robert S. Norris and Hans Kristensen, "Global Nuclear Weapons Inventories, 1945–2011," *Bulletin of the Atomic Scientists* 66, no. 4 (July/August 2011); and Kerr and Nikitin, 19–21.

[25] The most notable of these is from the International Institute of Strategic Studies, available at <www.iiss.org/publications/strategic-dossiers/nbm/nuclear-black-market-dossier-a-net-assesment/pakistans-nuclear-programme-and-imports-/>.

[26] Numbers derived from Robert S. Norris and Hans Kristensen, "Nuclear Notebook: Pakistan's Nuclear Forces 2007," *Bulletin of the Atomic Scientists*, May/June 2007, available at <www.fas.org/sgp/crs/nuke/RL34248.pdf>; Hans M. Kristensen and Robert S. Norris, "Pakistan's Nuclear Forces 2011," *Bulletin of the Atomic Scientists* 67, no. 4 (July 2011), 91–92, available at <http://bos.sagepub.com/content/67/4/91.full.pdf+html>.

[27] Norris and Kristensen, "Global Nuclear Weapons Inventories, 1945–2011," 83.

[28] Ibid., 82.

[29] For a recent detailed discussion of this "minimum deterrence" construct and its limitations, see Khan, "Minimum Deterrence," 46.

[30] For a review of this growing Pakistani commitment to smaller highly enriched uranium (HEU) nuclear warheads and those based on plutonium, see Tom Hundley, "Pakistan's terrible, horrible, no-good, very bad idea to develop battlefield nukes," *Foreign Policy.com*, September 5, 2012, available at <http://isis-online.org/isis-reports/detail/pakistan-doubling-rate-of-making-nuclear-weapons-time-for-pakistan-to-rever/>.

[31] Pakistan's growing plutonium production capability is documented in Stockholm International Peace Research Institute (SIPRI), *SIRPI Yearbook 2011: Armaments, Disarmament and International Security* (Oxford: Oxford University Press, 2011), 11; International Panel on Fissile Materials (IPFM), *Global Fissile Material Report 2011* (Princeton, NJ: IPFM, 2011), 11. Also see David Albright and Paul Brannan, "Pakistan doubling rate of making nuclear weapons: time for Pakistan to reverse course," Institute for Science and International Security (ISIS), May 16, 2011, available at <http://isis-online.org/isis-reports/detail/pakistan-doubling-rate-of-making-nuclear-weapons-time-for-pakistan-to-rever/>.

[32] These conclusions reflect those found in David O. Smith, *The U.S. Experience with Nuclear Weapons: Lessons for South Asia* (Washington, DC: The Stimson Center, March 2013), 2–3, available at <www.stimson.org/program-news/david-smith-on-tactical-nuclear-weapons-in-south-asia/>.

[33] Norris and Kristensen, "Global Nuclear Weapons Inventories, 1945–2011," 83.

[34] *Global Fissile Material Report 2010*, International Panel on Fissile Materials, available at <http://fissilematerials.org/library/gfmr10.pdf>, 131.

[35] Ibid., 132–133.

[36] See David Albright and Paul Brannan, "Pakistan Appears to Be Building a Fourth Military Reactor at the Khushab Nuclear Site," ISIS report, February 9, 2011; and Joby Warrick, "Nuclear Experts Say Pakistan May Be Building a 4th Plutonium Reactor," *The Washington Post*, February 9, 2011, available at <www.washingtonpost.com/wp-dyn/content/article/2011/02/09/AR2011020906388.html>.

[37] Once all four heavy water reactors come on line at Khushab, international experts estimate that Pakistan will be able to generate up to 50 kg of weapons-grade plutonium per year, nearly 2½ as much as it generates from two Khushab reactors today. See IPFM, *Pakistan Country Report*, February 3, 2013, available at <http://fissilematerials.org/countries/pakistan.html>. Like those at Kahuta, the nuclear facilities at Khushab are not subject to IAEA inspections. See FAS, *Weapons Around the World: Khushab/Khusab*, March 15, 2000, available at <www.fas.org/nuke/guide/pakistan/facility/khushab.htm>.

[38] Warrick.

[39] Details of Pakistan's ballistic and cruise missile developments since 2009 are found at Norris and Kristensen (July/August 2011); and at Bruno Tertrais, "Pakistan's Nuclear and WMD Programmes: Status, Evolution and Risks," *EU Non-Proliferation Consortium: Non-Proliferation Papers*, number 19, July 2012, 4, 6–8.

[40] Cited in "Pakistan Successfully Test Fires Hatf-9 Nasr Missile," *The Nation* (Pakistan), May 29, 2012, available at <www.nation.com.pk/pakistan-news-newspaper-daily-english-online/national/29-May-2012/pakistan-successfully-test-fires-hatf-9-nasr-missile>.

[41] Among several unspecified technical issues with the April 2011 Nasr missile test was the inability to fire multiple missiles from a launcher. These issues were reportedly rectified during late 2012 and early 2013 follow-on tests. See Shikander Shaheen, "Pakistan successfully test fires Hatf-IX missile," *The Nation* (Pakistan), February 12, 2003, available at <www.nation.com.pk/pakistan-news-newspaper-daily-english-online/national/12-Feb-2013/pakistan-successfully-test-fires-hatf-ix-missile>.

[42] Kristensen and Norris, "Pakistan's Nuclear Forces 2011," 93.

[43] Karen DeYoung, "New Estimates Put Pakistan's Nuclear Arsenal at More Than 100," *The Washington Post*, January 31, 2011; and Kristensen and Norris, "Pakistan's Nuclear Forces 2011," 93.

[44] The conclusion that Pakistan has attained the technical know-how for miniaturizing nuclear weapons, using both uranium and plutonium, is shared among analysts including Shaun Gregory in "Terrorist Tactics in Pakistan Threaten Nuclear Safety," *Combating Terrorism Center* (CTC) *Journal* 4, no. 6 (June 2011), 4; Tom Hundley; and by Pakistani observer Mansoor Ahmed as quoted in Smith, *The U.S. Experience with Nuclear Weapons*.

[45] See Michael Krepon, "Tactical Nukes in South Asia," *Arms Control Wonk—23 Comments*, April 18, 2012, available at <http://krepon.armscontrolwonk.com/archive/3419/tac-nukes-in-south-asia>.

[46] Pakistan's advances with small, plutonium-fueled (4–6 kg size) warheads provide it with nuclear weapons able to deliver yields of 3–5 kilotons (KT) of explosive impact. This is a major reduction in the explosive yield of most of Pakistan's uranium-based nuclear arsenal, which delivers less accurate and far larger target yields of 20–40 KT of explosive impact. For a review of the physics of nuclear weapons yield and small-yield plutonium-based weapons, see "Nuclear Weapons Design: Special Weapons Primer," Federation of American Scientists Web Site, available at <www.fas.org/nuke/intro/nuke/design.htm>.

[47] On the dynamic of signaling versus credibility in relation to U.S. military historic experience with battlefield nuclear weapons and the applicability to Pakistan, including his conclusion that "Rather than improving Pakistan's deterrence of India, these weapons hold only the promise of lowering the nuclear threshold and guaranteeing a larger nuclear exchange by both sides once they are used," see Smith, *The U.S. Experience with Nuclear Weapons*, 31–41. On the degree to which Pakistan's ambiguous and uncertain relationship with Islamic militants and terrorist organizations acting in Jammu-Kashmir and India render it a dubious "unitary actor" in the construct of nuclear weapons deterrence theory, see Perkovich, "The NonUnitary Model," 8–16.

[48] This is a frequently repeated statement from Pakistani nuclear officials; it was made in an off-the-record comment by a senior Strategic Plans Division official to author during a conference, February 2011.

[49] Such use is actually advocated in a proposal, published in fall 2011, by a Pakistani security consultant. See Maria Sultan, "Cold Start Doctrine and Pakistan's Counter-measures: Theory of Strategic Equivalence-III," *The News*, September 30, 2011, available at <www.thenews.com.pk/TodaysPrint-Detail.aspx?ID=70218&Cat=2>.

[50] Kristensen and Norris, "Pakistan's nuclear forces, 2011," 4–5. Also see the technical assessment of Pakistani University physicist Pervez Hoodbhoy: "The plutonium has no commercial purpose. Instead, the goal is to produce lighter but deadlier bombs to be fitted on to missile tips." Pervez Hoodbhoy, "Pakistan's rush for more bombs—why?" *The Express Tribune*, January 29, 2012, available at <http://tribune.com.pk/story/328922/pakistans-rush-for-more-bombs--why/>.

[51] See Vipin Naran, "Pakistan's Nuclear Posture: Implications for South Asian Stability," policy brief, Harvard Kennedy Center, Belfer Center for Science and International Affairs, January 2010.

[52] The great and growing risk of unintended battlefield use due to capability outpacing doctrinal thinking was made most compellingly by a former Pakistani nuclear weapons program leader, interviewed by author, November 2012.

[53] For a list and analysis of India's extensive number of major conventional weapons procurement programs and their expenses, see Stephen P. Cohen and Sunil Dasgupta, *Arming Without Aiming: India's Military Modernization* (New York: Penguin, 2010).

[54] India's plans to marry the nuclear-capable Sagarika ballistic missile and Arihant nuclear submarine fleet has been signaled by the Defense Research and Development Organization (DRDO) in a series of announcements coincident with the missile tests. See "K-15 Sagarika Missile successfully tested and set to join INS Arihant," *DefenceForumIndia.com*, December 28, 2012, available at <http://defence-forumindia.com/k-15-sagarika-successfully-tested-and-set-to-join-ins-arihant-1300>; and K.R. Bolton, "INS Arihant and India's Geopolitical Role," *Foreign Policy Journal* (India), August 15, 2012, available at <www.foreignpolicyjournal.com/2012/08/15/ins-arihant-and-indias-geopolitical-role/>. It is important to note that Indian estimates of weapons fielding timelines are notoriously unreliable and chronically overoptimistic. Delays induced by political and bureaucratic inertia, corruption, and general lethargy are more commonly present than not, and there is a history of postponing projected fielding dates back by up to a decade or more. For a discussion of this historic pattern, see Cohen and Dasgupta.

[55] Under development since 1996, the Prithvi-II is India's emerging long-range, mobile missile capable of firing conventional or nuclear payloads of 500 kg or less to a distance of 350 meters. It exceeds the older Prithvi-I in terms of range and accuracy. See "Prithvi-II Successfully Test Fired from Odisha," *The Hindu Online*, October 4, 2012, available at <www.opensource.gov/portal/server.pt/gate-way/PTARGS_0_0_200_219_998_43/content/Display/SAP20121004428003>.

[56] See "Pakistan test fires nuclear-capable short-range Hatf-IX Missile," *NDTV.com* (India), May 29, 2012, available at <www.ndtv.com/article/world/pak-test-fires-nuclear-capable-short-range-hatf-ix-missile-217235>; Hundley; Michael Krepon, "Unwarranted Assessments," *Dawn.com*, July 23, 2012, available at <http://dawn.com/2012/07/23/unwarranted-assessments/>, where he states in a fashion that is appealing to Pakistani publishers, "After this deal was struck, those who determine requirements for Pakistan's credible minimum deterrence began to emphasise credibility and de-emphasise minimalism. Three related developments in Pakistan after the deal are especially noteworthy: the construction of a fourth plutonium reactor to increase Pakistan's inventory of nuclear weapons, the

imposition of a veto on negotiations for a fissile-material cut-off treaty and the explicit requirement for battlefield, or tactical, nuclear weapons."

[57] The Indian antiballistic missile (ABM) radar systems are known as Green Pine and Swordfish, the former acquired directly from Israel and from its Arrow ABM system, and the Swordfish developed as an improved system capable of incorporating satellite data. See "The Indian Cure for Ballistic Missiles," *StrategyPage.com*, March 9, 2011, available at <www.strategypage.com/htmw/htada/20110309.aspx>.

[58] While some Indian security think tanks have called for India to move beyond a lukewarm program of testing ABM systems capable of defeating long-range attacking missiles, New Delhi remains far short of serious development and testing for a robust antimissile defense. The majority view in India's political and military circles does not favor pursuit of a viable antiballistic missile system at this point and seems unlikely to change without a challenge from China or elsewhere that might call its nuclear deterrence posture into question. For a summary of these dynamics, see Debak Das, "India: How Credible Is Its Ballistic Missile Defence?" India-Article #3768, November 29, 2012, available at <www.ipcs.org/article/india/india-how-credible-is-its-ballistic-missile-defence-3768.html>.

[59] This point made to the author by a former Pakistani nuclear weapons program leader who wished to remain anonymous during questioning in November 2012. It also aligns with the assessment of Stimson Center Pakistani nuclear arms expert Michael Krepon, "The Arms Crawl That Wasn't," *Arms Control Wonk*, November 7, 2011, available at <http://krepon.armscontrolwonk.com/archive/3265/the-arms-crawl-that-wasn%E2%80%99t>.

[60] For Iran's disclaimers about its nuclear weapons intentions, see Iran's paid advertisement, "An Unnecessary Crisis—Setting the Record Straight about Iran's Nuclear Program," *The New York Times*, November 18, 2005, A-11. Also see Ali Akbar Salehi, *A Conversation with Ali Akbar Salehi, Foreign Minister of Iran* (Washington, DC: Council on Foreign Relations, October 1, 2012), available at <www.cfr.org/iran/conversation-ali-akbar-salehi/p29197>. As discussed in note 2, the IAEA has stated that "Iran is not providing the necessary cooperation, including by not implementing its Additional Protocol," such that the agency is "unable . . . to conclude that all nuclear material in Iran is in peaceful activities." See *Implementation of the NPT Safeguards Agreement and relevant provisions of the Security Council resolutions in the Islamic Republic of Iran* (New York: IAEA Board of Governors, February 25, 2011), 7–8; and David Albright, Andrea Stricker, and Christina Walrond, *IAEA Iran Safeguards Report: Expansion of Natanz Enrichment Plant Lags; LEU Production Not as High as Expected; Iran Readying Advance Centrifuges for Deployment?; Continued Non-Cooperation on Military Dimensions [Rev. 1]* (Washington, DC, Institute for Science and International Security, February 25, 2011), 4. The IAEA has also cited aspects of Iran's nuclear program that make it look to have a military component: "The information indicates that Iran has carried out the following activities that are relevant to the development of a nuclear explosive device:

- Efforts, some successful, to procure nuclear related and dual use equipment and materials by military related individuals and entities (Annex, Sections C.1 and C.2);
- Efforts to develop undeclared pathways for the production of nuclear material (Annex, Section C.3);
- The acquisition of nuclear weapons development information and documentation from a clandestine nuclear supply network (Annex, Section C.4); and

- Work on the development of an indigenous design of a nuclear weapon including the testing of components (Annex, Sections C.5–C.12).

While some of the activities identified in the Annex have civilian as well as military applications, others are specific to nuclear weapons. The information indicates that prior to the end of 2003 the above activities took place under a structured programme. There are also indications that some activities relevant to the development of a nuclear explosive device continued after 2003, and that some may still be ongoing." See *Implementation of the NPT Safeguards Agreement and relevant provisions of Security Council resolutions in the Islamic Republic of Iran: A Director General's Report* (New York: IAEA Board of Governors, November 8, 2011), 8. Iran is believed to be aiming at attainment of a "breakout" capability, one where it would be able to make a nuclear weapon in a short period of time should it decide to do so. It is thus believed to be pursuing three components necessary for a usable nuclear weapon: highly enriched uranium, a device capable of initiating a nuclear explosion and a delivery vehicle. See Louis Hellman et al., "Fact Sheet: Iran's Nuclear and Ballistic Missile Programs," The Center for Arms Control and Non-Proliferation, January 2013, available at <http://armscontrolcenter.org/publications/factsheets/fact_sheet_irans_nuclear_and_ballistic_missile_programs/>.

[61] In regard to an envisioned U.S. invasion, see ibid., October 1, 2012: "We have many examples. Look at the Vietnam War. Look at other examples around. And look at . . . Saddam Hussein. I remember at the time we have so much difficulty in justifying our position . . . although it was clear . . . they would say, oh, you know, as the aggressor, Iran is so; Iran is that; Iran is the guilty party . . . but eventually everything was exposed. The reality was exposed to the entire international community, who was just, who was right and who was on the side of . . . righteousness and truth. And here we are, where Saddam is and where Iran is." Iranian Supreme Leader Ayatollah Ali Khamenei is also reported to believe that Libyan dictator Muammar Qadhafi's 2002 abandonment of his nuclear program made him vulnerable to the 2012 U.S./Western intervention that led to his overthrow. See Karim Sadjadpour and George Perkovich, "The Iranian Nuclear Threat," Carnegie Endowment for International Peace Issues Profile, November 29, 2012, available at <http://carnegieendowment.org/globalten/?fa=50140>.

[62] These aims roughly align with the three famously outlined in Scott D. Sagan, "Why Do States Build Nuclear Weapons? Three Models in Search of a Bomb," *International Security* 21, no. 3 (Winter 1996/1997), 54–86.

[63] Iranian Foreign Minister Salehi stated as much in October 2012: "Had Iran chosen to go nuclear, in the sense of weaponization, that certainly would not be deterrent for Iran. On the contrary, it would—I don't know what the opposite word is. It would attract more threat and invite more threat from the other side, because suppose we wanted to go nuclear and manufacture one or two rudimentary bombs. Who is on the other side? It's not India and Pakistan. Seemingly, it is Iran and the U.S. Can we ever be on equal footing with the U.S. in this regard? Does any rational person . . . think to challenge U.S., a country like Iran, nuclearwise? Certainly not, because if you have one or two bombs, you want to use it against whom? Who is our enemy?"

[64] See Vali Nasr, *The Shia Revival: How Conflicts Within Islam Will Shape the Future* (New York: Norton, 2006), 159–168.

[65] India has the third largest Shia minority in the world, estimated at between 9 and 14 percent of the global total in 2009. See "Mapping the Global Muslim Population: A Report on the Size and Distribution of the World's Muslim Population," The Pew Forum on Religion and Public Life, October 7, 2009, available at <www.pewforum.org/Muslim/Mapping-the-Global-Muslim-Population(6).aspx>.

[66] See reference to India-Iran strategic and military relationship in Kenneth Katzman, *Iran: U.S. Concerns and Policy Responses*, Report RL32048 (Washington, DC: Congressional Research Service, November 15, 2012), 25. It is worth observing that India has "strategic relations" with at least 42 countries. Thus, New Delhi's standard for strategic interaction with Iran is not consistent with a close alliance or even partnership.

[67] For support, see Lieutenant General Ronald L. Burgess, Jr., USA, director, Defense Intelligence Agency, "Iran's Military Power," statement before the Senate Committee on Armed Services, April 14, 2010, 13.

[68] Pervez Hoodhboy, "Iran's Bomb and Pakistan," *The Express Tribune*, January 15, 2012, available at <http://tribune.com.pk/story/321943/irans-bomb-and-pakistan/>.

[69] "Iran Doesn't Need Nuclear Weapons: Qureshi," *The Express Tribune*, October 19, 2012, available at <http://tribune.com.pk/story/64577/iran-doesnt-need-nuclear-weapons-qureshi/>.

[70] Ibid.

[71] Yousuf Raza Gilani, "Pakistan Not Bound by U.S. Sanctions on Iran," *The Nation* (Pakistan), June 22, 2010, available at <www.nation.com.pk/pakistan-news-newspaper-daily-english-online/Politics/22-Jun-2010/Pakistan-not-bound-to-US-sanctions-onIran-Gilani>.

[72] "India Doesn't Want Iran to Become a Nuclear State," *Daily Times,* September 17, 2005, available at <www.dailytimes.com.pk/print.asp?page=2005\09\17\story_17-9-2005_pg4_14>.

[73] Indrani Bagchi, "Resolve Syrian Conflict, Row over Nuclear Plan, Manmohan Singh to Tell Iran," *Times of India*, August 27, 2012, available at <http://articles.timesofindia.indiatimes.com/2012-08-27/india/33424191_1_president-mahmoud-ahmedinejad-iranian-supreme-leader-ayatollah-nam-summit>.

[74] Ironically, attaining status as a "virtual" nuclear state would put Iran in a status similar to that of Israel. But by keeping its nuclear weapons secret, Tehran would probably be limited to producing only a few weapons, and such a small arsenal might dissuade Iran from giving weapons to proxies for covert use, which in turn would undermine a major motivation for pursuing this scenario. While Iran might build nuclear weapons and keep them secret until it had accumulated a large enough stockpile to withstand a counterforce strike, that course of action is unlikely.

[75] As reported by James Risen and Mark Mazzetti, "U.S. Agencies See No Move by Iran to Build a Bomb," *The New York Times*, February 24, 2012, available at <www.nytimes.com/2012/02/25/world/middleeast/us-agencies-see-no-move-by-iran-to-build-a-bomb html?_r=0>. This 2010 assessment matches the 2003 assessment of Iranian pathways by Brookings Institution expert Ray Takeyh, in "Iran's Nuclear Calculations," *World Policy Journal* 20, no. 2 (Summer 2003), 21–28.

[76] Support for a political explanation of Iran's nuclear program is found in the observation of Mark Fitzpatrick, International Institute for Strategic Studies Nonproliferation and Disarmament Program, that if Iran had wanted to build a nuclear weapon as rapidly as possible, it could have produced fissile materials more quickly. The Federation of American Scientist's Ivan Oelrich agrees, arguing that the slow pace of Iran's low enriched uranium (LEU) activity shows the government is not pursing an

actual weapon. Israeli authorities have been quoted as saying that the Stuxnet virus set back Iran's nuclear ambitions considerably, and it will be 2015 before Iran can develop a bomb. Preparations for "break-out capacity" could include breaking down Iran's nuclear program into component parts distributed among civilian institutions such as universities and private companies (unclassified reports are that the 2007 U.S. National Intelligence Estimate states this began happening after 2003) and stockpiling LEU to speed up the production of HEU if needed. However, it might also pursue a plutonium weapon if it could build a secret reprocessing facility. This might be considered too risky (and too expensive) a venture, but it could be an attractive alternative to uranium enrichment programs, which have been complicated by sabotage and continue to rely on imported materials and components. Fitzpatrick argues that clandestine HEU production is the most likely route. See Mark Fitzpatrick, Assessing Iran's Nuclear Program Without Exaggeration or Complacency, Iran Nuclear Brief, The Arms Control Association, October 2, 2011, 3–4, available at <www.armscontrol.org/files/Iran_Brief_10_2011_Mark_Fitzpatrick.pdf>.

[77] Riedel observes that the security impact of such an Iranian outcome would be "in slow motion." See Bruce Riedel, *Iran-U.S. Relations After the Iranian Bomb* (Washington, DC: The Brookings Institution, September 30, 2011), 1.

[78] Nevertheless, there are some indications that Iran may be pursuing this avenue of nuclear development. If its nuclear program stopped at the point of break-out capacity, it would take months to retaliate to an attack with nuclear force. But recent developments in missile technology, including the new solid fuel Sajjil missile, suggest that Iran is pursuing (potentially nuclear) missile capabilities that could be deployed immediately in response to foreign aggression. While an undeclared nuclear capability would allow Iran to maintain its rhetorical rejection of nuclear force, an ambiguous capability like Israel's would serve as a strong deterrent. However, Iran cannot expect the international forbearance necessary to follow the Israeli model. See Bruno Tertrais, "A Nuclear Iran and NATO," *Survival* 52, no. 6 (November 2010), 45–62.

[79] For example see Riedel, *Iran-U.S. Relations After the Iranian Bomb*, 4–5.

[80] These stark possibilities as of 2012 are detailed in Karim Sadjadpour and George Perkovich, "The Iranian Nuclear Threat," Carnegie Endowment for International Peace Issues Profile, November 29, 2012, available at <http://carnegieendowment.org/globalten/?fa=50140>.

[81] Riedel, *Iran-U.S. Relations After the Iranian Bomb*, 4–5; and Christopher Clary and Mara E. Karlin, "The Pak-Saudi Nuke, and How to Stop It," *The American Interest*, July–August 2012.

[82] For a review of Saudi concerns over Iranian actions within Shia minority communities on the Arabian Peninsula during 2012, see Bruce Riedel, "Iran Seeks to Exploit Grievances of Saudi Arabian Shias," *Al-Monitor.com*, November 9, 2011, available at <www.al-monitor.com/pulse/originals/2012/al-monitor/iran-shia-saudi.html?utm_source=dlvr.it&utm_medium=twitter>.

[83] Saudi efforts to check Iranian hegemonic ambitions have included its active support since 1979 for opposition groups to Iran and its Shia-supported agents in Lebanon, Syria, Iraq, Bahrain, Kuwait, and elsewhere across the Middle East. See Nasr, *The Shia Revival*, 156–165, 222–242; "Saudi King Calls Islamic Summit," *RTT News, July 23, 2012, available at* <www.rttnews.com/1928093/saudi-king-calls-islamic-summit.aspx?type=gn&Node=B1>.

[84] For a more detailed discussion of the Saudi-American fallout over the wisdom of invasion and the ultimate disposition of Iraq in relation to Iran, see Nawaf Obaid, "Stepping Into Iraq,"

The Washington Post, November 29, 2006, available at <www.washingtonpost.com/wp-dyn/content/article/2006/11/28/AR2006112801277.html>; Suzanne Goldenberg, "If US leaves Iraq we will arm Sunni militias, Saudis say," *The Guardian* (UK), December 13, 2006, available at <www.theguardian.com/world/2006/dec/14/iraq.saudiarabia>; and Yoel Guzansky, "Iraq and the Arabs Following the American Withdrawal," *Strategic Assessment* 15, no. 3 (October 2012), 42–43.

[85] Presidential candidate Hillary Clinton first raised the possibility of extension of an American nuclear umbrella over the Middle East if Iran were to acquire nuclear weapons in 2008. As Secretary of State, she repeatedly warned that the United States would consider extending a "defense umbrella" over the Middle East if Iran did not halt its nuclear program. See Mark Landler and David E. Sanger, "Clinton Speaks of Shielding Mideast from Iran," *The New York Times*, July 22, 2009, available at <www.nytimes.com/2009/07/23/world/asia/23diplo.html>.

[86] Riedel, *Iran-U.S. Relations After the Iranian Bomb*, 6.

[87] Among these activities, the Kingdom signed a 2008 memorandum of understanding (MOU) with the United States promising American assistance with Saudi civil nuclear power on the condition that Riyadh does not pursue "sensitive nuclear technologies." Since then, the Saudis have expanded their options by signing nuclear cooperation agreements with France, South Korea, Argentina, and, in early 2012, China. Each of these agreements assures the Kingdom the right to enrich its own uranium—something not possible in the 2008 U.S.-Saudi MOU. Also see Hugh Tomlinson, "Saudi Arabia to Acquire Nuclear Weapons to Counter Iran, *The Times* (London), February 11, 2012, available at <www.theaustralian.com.au/news/world/saudi-arabia-to-acquire-nuclear-weapons-to-counter-iran/story-fnb64oi6-1226268171576>.

[88] "Saudi Plans to Build 16 Nuclear Reactors by 2030," Reuters-Africa, June 1, 2011, available at <http://af.reuters.com/article/energyOilNews/idAFLDE75004Q20110601>.

[89] Tomlinson.

[90] See Jason Burke, "Saudi Arabia Worries about Stability, Security and Iran," *The Guardian* (UK), June 29, 2011, available at <www.guardian.co.uk/world/2011/jun/29/saudi-arabia-prince-turki-arab-spring-iran>; and "Saudi Arabia May Need Nuclear Weapons to Fend Off Threat from Iran and Israel, Says Former Intelligence Chief," *Daily Mail* (UK), December 6, 2011, available at <www.dailymail.co.uk/news/article-2070704/Saudi-Arabia-need-nuclear-weapons-fend-threat-Iran-Israel-says-prince.html>. While Prince Turki's comments were in an unofficial capacity, they contrasted strongly to those he made as Saudi ambassador to Great Britain in 2003. See Turki al-Faisal, "No Nukes" letters, *The Guardian* (UK), September 22, 2003.

[91] The Saudis would also require an off-the-shelf missile purchase for any nuclear warheads because its current ballistic missile capability consists of aged and notoriously suspect Chinese CSS-2 "East Wind" missiles covertly purchased from Beijing and smuggled into the Kingdom in the 1980s. See Thomas Lippman, "Saudi Arabia: The Calculations of Uncertainty," in *The Nuclear Tipping Point*, ed. Kurt Campbell, Robert Einhorn, and Mitchell Reiss, 112–116 (Washington, DC: Brookings Institution Press, 2004. See also Tomlinson.

[92] The cited Saudi officials acknowledged that the official position of the Kingdom remains to see complete nuclear disarmament across the Middle East region, but it has privately concluded that Israel will never surrender its undeclared nuclear arsenal, making Riyadh determined to act in the event of an Iranian nuclear weapon. Ibid.

[93] Here I argue that growing Saudi concerns about Iran's nuclear possibilities and the unreliability of American support for the House of Saud, both of which have advanced markedly since the end of 2010, make an approach to Pakistan for nuclear weapons assistance far more likely than speculated in the pre-2010 writings of Lippman and Ibrahim al-Marashi. See Lippman, "Saudi Arabia," 111–141; and Ibrahim al-Marashi, "Saudi Petro-Nukes? Riyadh's Nuclear Intentions and Regime Survival Strategies," in *Forecasting Nuclear Proliferation in the 21st Century: A Comparative Perspective*, vol. 2, ed. William C. Potter, 76–99 (Stanford, CA: Stanford University Press, 2010).

[94] Riedel, *Iran-U.S. Relations After the Iranian Bomb*, 4–5.

[95] Husain Haqqani, *Pakistan: Between Military and Mosque* (Washington, DC: Carnegie Endowment for International Peace, 2005), 18.

[96] For example, see the discussion of some of these historic military connections in Bruce Riedel, "Saudi Arabia: Nervously Watching Pakistan," *Brookings Institution Opinion*, January 28, 2008, available at <www.brookings.edu/research/opinions/2008/01/28-saudi-arabia-riedel>.

[97] Concerning Pakistan's reliance on loans and energy credits to fund its nuclear program, see Riedel, "Saudi Arabia: Nervously Watching Pakistan," January 28, 2008; and Khan, *Eating Grass*, 171–172. Also see "Saudi Arabia country profile," *SIPRI Update*, July 2004, available at <http://archives.sipri.org/contents/expcon/cnsc2sau.html>.

[98] See the brief description of Saudi support for Pakistani nuclear weapons development in tandem with multiple Pakistani political and military leaders from Ali Bhutto in the 1970s to President Pervez Musharraf in 2003 in ibid.; see also Tomlinson; and Khan, *Eating Grass*, 172.

[99] Confronted with world sanctions if it responded to India's May 1998 nuclear tests with its own, Saudi Arabia promised Pakistan 50,000 barrels of free oil per day. Pakistan relied on this oil commitment and other large investments from various Saudi Princes and Saudi religious institutions to weather the American and Western economic sanctions that followed Pakistan's May 1998 response test. Riedel, "Saudi Arabia"; and Tomlinson.

[100] See "Saudis 'Mull Buying Nukes from Pakistan,'" UPI.com Special Reports, July 25, 2012, available at <www.upi.com/Top_News/Special/2012/07/25/Saudis-mull-buying-nukes-from-Pakistan/UPI-94601343239152/>; and Senator Sehar Kamran, *Pak-Gulf Defense and Security Cooperation*, Center for Pakistan and Gulf Studies (CPGS)—Occasional Paper (Rawalpindi: CPGS, January 2013), 7. For more on the history of this long-rumored nuclear bilateral arrangement see Riedel, "Saudi Arabia: Nervously Watching Pakistan"; and "Saudi Arabia country profile."

[101] See Kamran, 7–8.

[102] For a discussion of Saudi nuclear weapons infrastructure limitations and the political liabilities it would seek to avoid from going "nuclear" in response to Iranian acquisition of the bomb, see al-Marashi; and the slightly dated but useful Thomas W. Lippman, "Saudi Arabia: The Calculations of Uncertainty," in *The Nuclear Tipping Point: Why States Reconsider Their Nuclear Choices*, ed. Kurt M. Campbell, Robert J. Einhorn, and Mitchell B. Reiss, 111–144 (Washington, DC: Brookings Institution, 2004).

[103] For a recitation of this interpretation of the Nuclear Non-Proliferation Treaty (NPT) regarding Saudi Arabia and Pakistan, see Clary and Karlin.

[104] For a detailed assessment, see Gregory Gause III and Toby C. Jones, "Saudi Arabia in the New Middle East," transcript, Council on Foreign Relations, January 26, 2012, available at <www.cfr.org/saudi-arabia/saudi-arabia-new-middle-east/p27205>.

[105] In this context, a specific extension of U.S. nuclear deterrence in a commitment to defend Saudi Arabia from a nuclear weapons threat by Iran is believed necessary because the Kingdom is one of many nonnuclear adherents to the 1968 NPT who doubt the relevance of the 1968 United Nations Security Council resolution by the United States, United Kingdom, and Soviet Union to defend any nonnuclear weapons state from attack or threat by nuclear weapons. For a summary of that declaration made in conjunction with the conclusion of the NPT, see statement by William C. Foster, "United States, United Kingdom and Soviet Union Propose Security Assurances Resolution," *Department of State Bulletin*, March 25, 1968, 401–403; and Ambassador Arthur Goldberg, "Statement of June 17 before the UN Security Council," *Department of State Bulletin*, July 8, 1968, 56–59.

[106] Former Pakistani nuclear weapons program leader, interview with author, November 2012.

[107] Although Retired Pakistani General Feroz Khan contends that Pakistan had a lot more to do with its own nuclear weapons designs than it is commonly given credit for, he also acknowledges China's pivotal role in sustaining and advancing Pakistan's nuclear fuel acquisition and weapons design know-how in the face of international isolation from the mid-1970s onward. See Khan, *Eating Grass*, 174–175, 195. A more extensive China-Pakistan relationship is asserted in multiple other sources, including Rodney Jones, *Nuclear Escalation Ladders in South Asia*, Defense Threat Reduction Agency Advanced Systems and Concepts Office Report Number ASCO 2011-007, April 2011, 19–21; and one of a series of scathing Indian think tank critiques found in Siddharth Ramana, "China-Pakistan Nuclear Alliance: An Analysis," IPCS monograph, August 2011.

[108] Clary and Karlin.

[109] Saudi Arabia acceded to the 1968 NPT in October 1988. Pakistan is a non-signatory and steadfast opponent. See "Signatories and Parties to the Treaty on the Non-Proliferation of Nuclear Weapons," *Bulletin of the Federation of American Scientists*, December 3, 1998, available at <www.fas.org/nuke/control/npt/text/npt3.htm>.

[110] See Khan, *Eating Grass*, 360–363.

[111] Ibid., 212–213, for development of this line of reasoning.

[112] The continuing relevance of the minimum provocation of Israel "imperative" was confirmed by a longtime Pakistani nuclear weapons insider who wished to remain anonymous, author interview, November 2012.

[113] For a detailed discussion of the misdirection of American strategic attention in South Asia, see Thomas F. Lynch III, *The 80% Solution: The Strategic Defeat of bin Laden's al-Qaeda and Implications for South Asian Security* (Washington, DC: The New America Foundation, February 2012), especially 10–16.

[114] Some of this educational work has begun. It should be encouraged and expanded and include a more frank discussion of past American misanalysis of limited nuclear war.

[115] Thomas Schelling, *Arms and Influence* (New Haven: Yale University Press, 1966), 47.

[116] On the importance of a continuing American military presence in the Gulf, see Clary and Karlin.

[117] See Khan, *Eating Grass*, 212–213, for development of this line of reasoning.

About the Author

Dr. Thomas F. Lynch III is a Distinguished Research Fellow in the Center for Strategic Research, Institute for National Strategic Studies, at the National Defense University (NDU). He focuses on South Asia, the Near East, and counterterrorism. He researches, writes, lectures, and organizes workshops and conferences for Department of Defense customers on the topics of Pakistan, Afghanistan, India, and the Subcontinent, the Gulf Arab states, and the past and future trajectory of radical Islam. He has published widely on these topics, including articles in *Orbis*, *The American Interest*, and *Joint Force Quarterly*; book chapters in publications by NDU Press and Johns Hopkins University Press; and feature monographs with the New America Foundation, Combating Terrorism Center at West Point, and NDU Press. Dr. Lynch joined NDU in July 2010 after a 28-year career as an Active-duty U.S. Army officer, serving in a variety of command and staff positions as an armor/cavalry officer and as a senior level politico-military analyst. Dr. Lynch holds a B.S. from the United States Military Academy and an MPA, M.A., and Ph.D. in International Relations from the Woodrow Wilson School of Public & International Affairs at Princeton University.

Dr. Lynch wishes to acknowledge the inspiration for this monograph provided from panelists and participants at the May 2011 NDU Symposium on Nuclear Proliferation and Crisis Stability on the Subcontinent. He also wishes to thank a series of dedicated research interns for their invaluable assistance in building and refining this text: Adelia Saunders, Iman Malik and Enoch Song.